Start a Cake Business:

At Home, in a Commercial Kitchen, or in a Retail Cake Shop

InformationTree Press

Middlebury VT, USA

Edited by: Paula Spencer

ISBN-13: 978-0-9816469-7-8

Printed in the United States of America.

Contents

1
INTRODUCTION

You Can Do It!

Perhaps you've been told by friends and family that you should go into business for yourself because of the scrumptious cakes you make for holiday and birthday celebrations. Perhaps it's simply been your dream to provide delectable desserts to the people in your community and be involved with the special events that occur in people's lives. Or, maybe you are a creative person and cake decorating is the perfect medium for you to express yourself. Many others, from celebrity pastry chefs to small-town cake shop owners, started the same way. Whatever your reason, it is possible to start and run a successful cake business, either part-time or full-time. Make no mistake, it does take a great deal of time, planning, dedication, and commitment, but you can do it! This book concisely summarizes what we've learned over the years and offers practical advice to entrepreneurs on what it means to own and operate a cake business. While a cake business seems like a much more manageable undertaking than a full-scale bakery, the specialized niche means that your choices on the small details of your operation matters more. Our goal is to provide a strong foundation in the initial details of starting your cake business.

Before getting started, a few things about the scope of this book and its intended audience:

This is a book with an emphasis on starting a legal small business either at home, in a shared kitchen or commercial bakery. If you are located in a community where cottage food production is legal, then nearly every chapter, other than the one on opening a cake shop, is specifically directed to you. If you live somewhere where selling food made at home is illegal, then the general principles of the book are still relevant for you, but should be interpreted in the context of a licensed baking environment, not the home.

While we offer sample recipes and advice for efficient business baking, this is not a cake decorating book or recipe book. Most people arrive at starting a cake business with their own recipes and strategies. Our goal is to reinforce a few tips and tricks we've learned along the way for those new to cake decorating on a deadline and those new to maximizing profit.

For those with a passion for learning, the patience to follow a multi-sequential business process and the tenacity to persevere when things are tough, an independent cake businesses can be very profitable. While competition has increased in recent years, the demand for cakes made by an individual or small shop, rather than a factory, grocery store, or wholesale club, has never been higher. Independent cake artists are able to provide more one-on-one specialized attention for their clients and are often willing to take on designs and ideas that commercial bakeries would not. The so-called "cake ladies" of the past are being superseded by today's cake-artists and sculptors creating every imaginable design and flavor combination. The popularization of the sugar arts by reality television shows such as Ace of Cakes, Cake Boss, Amazing Wedding Cakes and others, means that no matter where you live, there is a greater awareness of and demand for great cakes. Coupled with the rise in demand for cupcakes, cake-pops, and homemade baked goods, there's never been a better time to start a cake business. Your decision to open a cake business may come from many reasons. It can be the perfect endeavor because it offers freedom: artistic freedom, freedom to work at the level that suits your lifestyle, freedom to raise your children without constant daycare, and the financial freedom that has come from building a reputable business offering a quality product.

You may have a lot of reasons for deciding to open a cake business. It may be your desire not only to earn a good living, but also to achieve greater personal satisfaction. Entrepreneurs in general, but especially food-oriented business people, often start out by watching and admiring others who are willing to take on the risk of self-employment. We can learn so much by observing and interacting with other businesses to discover what works. Then, through research, planning, and perseverance, we let go of the limits holding us back and embrace the potential for greater success. While any bakery business includes long hours and personal sacrifice, a cake business is a very specific niche, enabling the owner to employ strategies that can streamline production and efficiency.

While this is a great business, it should be noted right up front that there are some challenging aspects to starting any business. The ability to bake tasty and beautiful cakes is not a guarantee of commercial success. Knowing how to decorate cakes and starting a business are two different things. Like any new start-up, cake decorating does require a commitment of your time, energy, and finances. Additionally, these changes may be an adjustment with which your family may have an initial hesitancy accepting. You will want to discuss all of your plans and have the full support of your family before undertaking this new career. Spouses are particularly important to have on board, wholeheartedly. The last thing you want is someone who disapproves, or is bringing negative energy into your business. Coming to an understanding about the realistic expectations of everyone involved—from the children (if you have kids) to the family pets, everyone needs to be aware of the possible changes taking place.

Your family's support is probably the most important factor if you are considering this as a home business. They will be directly affected by your business. As Earlene Moore points out, most birthday parties, special celebrations, and weddings are held on the weekends. This may mean that you are not available to your family at all times, including during their leisure time. Advance planning and keeping a calendar of events is a must to avoid conflicts during those really important family occasions and commitments. Most successful entrepreneurs will tell you that they never could have made it if their family wasn't 100% supportive. Sure, there will be times when your work gets in the way of family time and this can cause tension, but overall, you want and need a supportive environment. Without it, your business will fail. Balancing a home business and family life can be achieved by following a few principles:

Communication – In order to secure and maintain the support of your family it is so important to keep the lines of communication open. As cliché as it may sound, no one can read your mind about what your expectations and needs are. Likewise, members of your family should be able to discuss their concerns and fears with you. For example, take the time upfront to explain what you are doing in your business and why certain sanitary conditions in the kitchen are critical to your success. Educate your family about the time you will need to concentrate on decorating or the noise level that must be maintained when the phone rings.

Clearly defined boundaries – If you are able to bake from home, your family kitchen will double as your place of business. Try to set up clear rules about what is off limits and when "business hours" should be observed. While a kitchen is a family resource, you need your business activities to be respected and your products to be safe. If possible, try to keep a regular schedule for baking and decorating. It is important to spend quality time with your family, relax and to get away from the "office" on occasion. This is particularly challenging for home-based bakers.

Keep finances separate – We will cover this in much greater detail, but family harmony requires that you keep separate bank accounts.

Involve your family – Obviously your family has a vested interest in your success! Keep them informed of your achievements and not just your challenges. If there are any tasks in which family members can participate, involve them. Among other things, they might help fold cake boxes, stamp envelopes, or conduct online research.

The Best Parts of Running a Cake Business

Happy customers – A cake brings a range of emotions – joy, pleasure, nostalgia – to so many people and will often be at the center of your customers' celebrations.

Personal expression – As a business owner, you can unleash your creativity and develop not only a delicious, handmade product, but also an experience that reflects your own personality.

Community Connection – You will become a vital member of your community. Both your customers and those with whom your cakes are shared, will appreciate the high-quality ingredients, custom flavors, and unique pleasure that comes from a handmade cake. As communities across the U.S. and worldwide look to recover from the economic damage of the past few years, many places will see a surge in small business efforts--individual entrepreneurs who recognize that building a vibrant community requires unique flavor and experiences easily distinguished from the massive homogeneous chain stores. This movement away from big box stores toward small, sustainable, and locally produced products is witnessed in the baking industry. The impact has been an increase in revenues in the U.S. bakery industry to more than $34 billion annually, according to the business research and consulting firm Frost & Sullivan.

Building a Brand – As a specialty cake producer, you are uniquely positioned to succeed. Consider the explosion of boutique food niches within the market: there are now more small food producers, farmers' markets, home-based "cottage" bakers, internet-only outlets, artisan providers, etc., than ever before. What's remarkable about all of these new niche operations is that while they are competition for traditional bakers, they are actually good for aspiring businesses. The trend toward small, handmade, unique, and wholesome baked goods is due in part to the greater availability of these products in the marketplace.

A Change of Pace – There's also a very enticing, lifestyle-changing profit potential. There will always be a growing demand for cakes. Two of the target consumers for cakes are couples and food aficionados. They are eager to find and share new culinary experiences, and are perpetual opportunities. Cakes are prefect for birthdays (everyone has one), bridal or baby showers, corporate events, or almost any type of gathering.

Lower Risk – With very few major national competitors operating in the United States, the sales opportunities for local operations are virtually limitless. Even with a challenging economic climate, people will still spend money on a handmade cake, particularly a wedding cake.

Working at Home – If permitted in your community, a home cake business can be ideal for stay-at-home parents because you probably have established many networks and relationships with other families: carpools, school groups, Girl or Boy Scout meetings, athletics teams, etc. Each one of these associations is filled with potential clients.

The Worst Parts of Running a Cake Business

Blood Sweat and Tears – Delivering your masterpiece to a wedding reception or party is just the pinnacle in a long sequence of difficult (at times) tasks. Operating a cake business is extremely hard work that is often romanticized in the media. Running a cake business means long days of waking up early to prepare ingredients, repair equipment, check on orders, order supplies, etc. There will also be late nights cleaning up, balancing books, marketing, and much more.

Unknown Unknowns – While most of the people we've met in this business are friendly, there is always the potential for conflict, whether it is from your competitors or your clients. Each new day in a cake business brings new challenges and a wide range of interactions. The best policy is to stay cool and have a script (a plan of what you will say) in a variety of situations.

No Excuses – Day-to-day, you can never know what to expect and because you're the boss, the challenges fall on your shoulders. There will always be life's little accidents, including broken equipment, power outages, running out of critical ingredients, meticulous health inspections, impossible client expectations, and never enough money. You've got to deal with it.

Working at Home – Keep in mind that working at home can also be very challenging with children nearby, seeking your attention and distracting you from your work. Try to balance the romantic visions of working at home, with the reality of getting actual work done.

Home Business Limitations – Whether it is the cottage food law restrictions on income or the size of your kitchen that will impact your ability to grow, the revenue that can be generated in a home operation is not easily scalable over time.

Get Rich Slowly – There is money to be made in the cake business, but it's certainly not a get rich quick scheme. A home cake business requires less capital, so it's easier to get started, but this is a labor intensive, one product at a time effort.

While the bakery industry as a whole continues to thrive, individual businesses come and go very quickly, often not surviving the first year. This book has been designed to provide you with the most up-to-date information possible to help ensure your success, giving you the tools and education which, when partnered with your motivation, business savvy, and a tasty product, will help you rise above the competition.

Few other feelings compare to the pride of owning a business, yet it can be tough and stressful. Make a list of pros and cons for yourself. Be very honest about your own personality in terms of motivation, your willingness to work unusual hours, budget management, organization, etc. and weigh the benefits with the inconveniences. Regardless of whether you chose to open a home-based-business, lease a shared kitchen, or invest in a commercial location, for most people, the benefits of owning their own business will far exceed the initial challenges. Remember, you're not the first person to do this, so there are many resources on which you can rely. The specialty food service is a multi-BILLION dollar industry. Whether you choose to specialize in retail orders sold from home or to diversify your offerings to include wholesale relationships such as catering, restaurant clients, or other special events, there is plenty of opportunity for a cake business to succeed. In the following chapters, everything from design ideas and equipment decisions, to building a client base and financial considerations will be explained in detail.

2
WORKING AT HOME

Legalities and Options

If your state permits a home cake business, this is a great opportunity to test the waters with very little overhead. That said, there are different types of home bakery businesses, each with varying degrees of regulatory requirements and you should be clear about what is legal in your community. The three types of home cake businesses we will cover in this book are those regulated by cottage food laws, where one can use their family kitchen to produce food for sale; home businesses with a separate licensed kitchen; and cake businesses where all business activity except food production takes place in the home.

If at all possible, we recommend starting out at home with your existing kitchen, as it is a safer way (financially) to explore this business. This is particularly true if you are already employed but dream of transitioning out of your existing job and into entrepreneurship. Most home businesses are started under cottage food laws. Cottage food production is when a person uses their family kitchen to produce foods for sale to the general public. These foods are made from Non-Potentially Hazardous Recipes and therefore not all baked goods are included in these regulations. For example, cheesecake, meringues, lemon curd, and many cream cheese frostings are prohibited. Cottage foods laws differ from state to state but typically involve limits on the types of foods produced, (nonhazardous) the annual amount of revenue, labeling requirements, inspection requirements, and other rules and regulations.

The Home Bakery Option

While a home bakery has some great benefits, it should be noted that there are some basic questions to consider before getting started. First off, is your kitchen up to the task of producing cakes and cupcakes for sale? Does your oven bake evenly? Can you count on your fridge and freezer to handle both your family's food as well as the raw ingredients for your products? Do you have enough of and the right kind of space for each part of the cake/

cupcake production-line including storage, mixing, baking, cooling, decorating, and business tasks? What areas might need some investment? Can you implement the strict food safety practices just as if you were in a commercial bakery? Is your family ok with the changes?

Consider each of these questions carefully, but don't let them discourage you if additional planning is required. There are many ways to tackle these challenges -- the best of which is being organized. Here are a few simple guidelines to keep in mind when organizing your home based bakery:

Paperwork and start-up processes take time to research and complete. Starting a business should be considered a marathon, not a sprint.

Set the ground-rules with your family about when/how the kitchen is being used for business and the expectations around food safety, the risks of contamination, and what items are off-limits for consumption (such as the batch of cupcakes for tomorrow's office party delivery). Adhering to the highest standards of food safety may be as simple as educating yourself and others about the health issues and consequences of improper food handling. Or, it may require you to set up a few constraints about how the kitchen is used during your 'business hours'.

Where possible, keep personal/family resources separate from business. This includes both financial resources like your checking account and credit cards, but also food and business supplies. For example, you don't want to mix family groceries with your cake ingredients. A simple way to avoid any mix-up is to designate shelves in your refrigerator or pantry as "business." Then, family members or housemates know not to use the items on these shelves.

All ingredients and supplies should be identified with a label of the contents and the date placed into use. In Chapter 11 we will cover in more detail the issues of food handling and storage.

If storage is a premium, consider investing in professional storage solutions for your pantry or cupboards. Alternatively, re-organize the existing storage in adjacent spaces. For example, a coat closet might be converted into storage for non-food items such as cake boards, boxes, and other paper supplies. A second refrigerator in the basement or garage is also a common investment.

While you may need to be creative, food and other perishable ingredients must always be stored off the ground, in the kitchen, fridge, or pantry. It is also important that you not store ingredients on the floor or in areas of warmth or moisture. Storage conditions should be dry, cool, and dark. Ideally, the temperature in any storage area should be 50 to 70 degrees Fahrenheit. Higher temperatures speed up deterioration. Always store foods in the coolest cabinets away from the range, oven, water heater, dishwasher, or any hot pipes. For example, the area under the sink is not a good place. Proper food storage is important to the health of your customers and your business.

Even in the smallest kitchens, a kitchen cart can keep you organized. Here, you'll keep your small wares such as measuring cups, spoons, pastry bags, and tips. You can even keep key ingredients in it such as baking soda and powder, food coloring, vanilla extract, meringue powder, fondants, and anything specialized for cake baking and decorating. While it might seem to be such a simple step, there can be no mistake that your cart is "off-limits" to everyone else in the family/household. Moreover, many kitchen carts have drop leaves for extra counter space and the cart can always be moved out of the way when it is time to return the kitchen back to the family domain.

Home Business: Beyond the Basics

Once you have determined that a cottage food/home cake business is permitted in your community, you still need to determine if local zoning laws are also a factor. It is better to be proactive rather than wait until a neighbor telephones local authority and complains that you have started a business in your home. Often, the primary issue is clients picking up cakes at your home, thereby taking up parking space on your street. It only takes one time that a neighbor is inconvenienced for that first call to the zoning authority. There are a few ways to address this situation:

1. Only offer delivery

2. Only allow pickup by appointment (so as to control parking).

3. Contact your local planning authority and alert them to your business activity before any conflict with your neighbor arises. They will provide guidance and address any restrictions on your property use.

If there are restrictions on your property, don't fret. First of all, people start businesses every day from their home. Municipalities recognize the value of new business growth and are almost always willing to work with you and your neighbors to resolve disagreements. Secondly, enforcement of minor zoning infractions is costly to city governments. They would much rather collect taxes from you, the business owner, while still resolving neighborhood skirmishes.

Mortgage – Another factor of starting a business at home is the possible restriction from your mortgage lender. Do not stick your head in the sand and avoid this possible problem. Again, shining the light of day on what you're doing is always the best course of action.

Insurance – As with your mortgage lender, your insurance company needs to know if you are operating a business at home and the possible liabilities resulting from your efforts. Again, avoiding this truth will only cause you problems down the road. Alert your agent of your activities and get a consultation on the changes that may be required to your policy.

Setting Up Your Home Office – Even if you cannot bake from home, you can set up a home office and run the non-food production aspects of your business. In order to take advantage of the tax benefits, your home office must be a space used exclusively for business activity. The IRS is very serious about the limited use of a home office to the point there can be no indication of other activity (kids doing homework, ironing board, dog crate). In the unlikely event you are audited for a home office, you may have to provide photographs of the space. Should there be any sign of non-business activity you could be in deep doo-doo (That is, loss and deduction and penalty with interest).

Communication – The lifeline of your business will be your computer and your phone. I strongly recommend that you keep personal and business communication expenses separate. If at all possible, a separate computer, e-mail account, Facebook page, and phone line should be used for your business. When you're first getting started, you might consider a Google Voice account as your business phone number. Google Voice is a unique business phone number but it rings your regular landline or cell phone. There are other inexpensive ways to procure a second phone number without investing in a dedicated business line.

Computer – As a business owner, your job is not only baking, but marketing, customer service, operations management, and more. A reliable computer and Internet connection are essential.

Use the following checklist when setting up your home office:

Adequate desk or work station

Comfortable & supportive office chair

Good lighting

Adequate storage

Sufficient electrical outlets

Printer

Fax

Scanner

Answering machine

Webcam

Other:

Can't Bake at Home?

Chapter 10 is entirely dedicated to getting legal, but what if your community does not allow cakes produced in a home kitchen to be sold to the public? Cake decorators are increasingly working to pass cottage food laws in places where home bakery businesses are illegal. You will find other bakers from your community organizing on websites or social networks to collect petition signatures, generate media attention, and lobby with local legislators. The legal process can be slow, and the cottage laws are still restrictive. Limits are often placed on the kinds of products that can be sold, as well as the total revenue that can be generated. Currently in Michigan for example, home bakers must cap their annual revenue at $15,000. Other cottage laws prevent advertising of any kind other than word-of-mouth. Of course, baking at home legally under cottage restrictions is still a great way to test the waters of this business.

Another approach that may be more sustainable in the long run is finding an alternative location (a health-inspected, legal kitchen) from which to do your baking and decorating. Often the only requirement to renting space in a shared kitchen is having your food handler's license. This course takes about a half-day to complete and is invaluable in preparing you to keep your customers safe from food-borne illness.

While your entire operation is not home-based, you can still run many of the business activities such as bookkeeping, marketing, client correspondence, etc., from your home office. Remember, as a business owner, there is much more work to do than just baking and decorating. There are multiple options available should you choose to work from a kitchen outside of your home.

Should you determine that you need a kitchen space outside of the home, you will want to consider the following qualities when evaluating spaces:

- Age and size of the oven(s)
- Availability of locked storage space
- Refrigerator space
- Hours of access
- Safety of the neighborhood/location
- Access to a loading dock
- Up-to-date health inspection/legal documentation

Shared Kitchen – Also known as kitchen incubators, shared kitchens are fully licensed, commercial kitchens, available for rent on an hourly, weekly, or even long-term basis. The concept has grown in recent years as the demand for professional food preparation space has exploded because of food entrepreneurs just like you. You will need to do some research into the equipment and storage options available to you as conditions vary from business to business. Many rental kitchens come equipped with quality professional equipment and onsite cold and dry storage. Others maintain accounts with wholesale distributors for all of your food and supply needs. With bulk purchasing power, ingredients may be less expensive. If a home-based cake business is illegal and you're not ready to renovate your home or get into a long term lease, renting a shared kitchen is the fastest way to establish yourself.

Alternatives to shared kitchens – Community Facilities For many people just starting out in the cake business, the economics of renting a shared kitchen doesn't make sense; yet, they are unable to bake legally from home. In these situations, we recommend looking for kitchen facilities in community buildings such as schools, places of worship (church or synagogue), Elks club, private schools, day care, senior center, etc. While this advice is commonly given on websites and cake decorating forums, we've found that little bit of preparation goes a long way. For example, do you have any connections with decision makers in these organizations? Can you provide your own insurance so there's no risk to the renting party? Draw up a formal written agreement that makes it simple for the facility to understand what you wish to do, the limits of their liability, as well as their responsibilities.

Use of a retail kitchen part time – If you are tuned into your local food community, you may be able to negotiate with a small business owner who already has a legal kitchen and would be amenable to renting out part-time. The key here is finding a business for whom a licensed kitchen is a necessity, but not in use for large blocks of time. For example, a cheese market may make fresh bread each morning, but then the kitchen sits idle. You might propose renting their space in those off-peak hours. Other ideas include markets or specialty shops where food is prepared, a catering business, a restaurant with limited hours, or a food-coop that offers week-end workshops or classes. Another approach is to partner with a shop or cafe that has available kitchen space but does not offer cake. In exchange for your fresh baked treats, you can also prepare your own products for sale to your week-end customers (weddings).

No matter where you ultimately find kitchen space for your cake business, do not lose sight of the ultimate conditions you seek.

The space must be licensed by local health officials, or if inspections are out of date, the space must pass inspection prior to the first month's rent. A copy of the certification should be provided with your lease or rental agreement. If you have any concerns about the validity of a venue's health inspection status, call your local health department for confirmation.

The space must have basic equipment, services, and satisfactory working conditions such as HVAC, security, and ideally, cold and dry storage. You don't want to rent a space only to find out it is too uncomfortable, too unsafe, etc. to actually work there.

You will also need access to the space for enough time and suitable hours to meet your business requirements.

An agreement in writing that spells out the terms of your use of the space should detail the rent, duration, timeline for payment (e.g. by the 30th of the month), and termination; the hours you have access to the space; the conditions in which the space will be kept and a breakdown of responsibility for utilities, repairs, insurance, security, etc.

Agreements

If you are paying to use someone else's space, you must get an agreement in writing. A written agreement protects both you and the owner. I can think of no reason for a landlord to object to a written agreement. Anyone who objects to a lease (even a month-to-month agreement) should raise suspicion. I've heard of too many good people put in difficult situations and put out of business because they did not have the legal protection of a written agreement.

3
EDUCATION

In 2009, the Conference Board Research Group reported that only 45% of Americans were satisfied with their work, dropping from 49% in 2008. The data recorded were the lowest in more than 22 years of studying the issue. It is no surprise given that most employees cannot count on their employers for the same security and benefits as previous generations. In turn, entrepreneurship is on the rise.

To some, entrepreneurship may seem more risky than having a "steady job", but I would argue that taking your career and livelihood into your own hands is less risky than handing your destiny over to someone else.

The following chapters will explain in detail, everything from recipe ideas and equipment decisions, to building a client base and time management tips. Regardless of whether you are an expert cake decorator or you simply have a desire to run a bakery, this book is written for the hands-on entrepreneur -- someone with a dream and the desire to work in the day-to-day operation of a cake business. In any food-service business, two of the most important aspects of the operation are product creation and the management of the business. Most people who start bakeries from the ground up aren't business people; they're what *E-Myth* author Michael E. Gerber calls "technicians" (i.e., people with a skill). For example, they can be people who love to make pies and want to reap the profits of their skill. If your cake business is to survive, you need both technical and business skills. The first key to success is to recognize where you need help and seek further education.

Let's start with the technical role: the baker. What are the qualifications to be a baker in a real cake business? Many entrepreneurs have started successful bakeries with little or no formal training; however, it is important for you or someone on staff to have a core set of competencies to run this business. The following self-assessment should help you understand if you need further experience or training.

Self-Evaluation

Communication

- Do you communicate effectively with others?
- Are you good at problem solving, asking questions to seek advice, and clarifying information?
- Could you write workplace manuals or procedures to train employees and standardize the business?
- Do you have a strong attention to detail?

Team Building

- Do you have experience as a leader?
- Can you build teams by setting and evaluating goals?
- Can you motivate people to complete tasks as defined by you, on time and to your standards?

Mathematical Concepts

- Are you able to make estimates of routine workplace measures such as weights, temperatures, and times?
- Are you able to use basic arithmetic processes?
- Are you able to notice mathematical errors and provide calculations to make corrections?

Food Safety

- Are you familiar with basic food safety practices for personnel, clothing, and equipment?
- Have you completed food handlers training?
- Can you maintain the work area in a clean and orderly state to meet health department standards?

Product Sourcing

- Are you comfortable locating and negotiating with vendors to supply ingredients?
- Are you able to recognize quality and fair prices when sourcing products?
- Are you able to identify products that do not meet quality requirements and rectify supply chain errors?

Customer Interaction

- Are you an outgoing person and a good listener?

- Are you able to interact with customers in a professional, courteous manner; handle complaints sensitively and with discretion; and take follow-up action as necessary to ensure customer satisfaction?
- Are you good at recognizing verbal and non-verbal cues to interpret someone's needs or concerns?

Functional Tasks

- Do you know how to use a computer? Point-of-sale equipment? Cash Register? Accounting software?
- Are you comfortable explaining computer applications to others? Could you install software, operate a website, and interact with vendors and customers online?
- Can you lift heavy ingredients, work in extreme hot or cold conditions, and safely maneuver in a potentially hazardous environment?
- Are you able to clean and sanitize equipment to meet health code requirements, prepare equipment for operation after cleaning, and keep accurate records of your process?
- Have you ever prepared and managed a large event (catering, large orders, etc.)?

Production

- Do you know how to measure supplies to confirm enough ingredients are available to meet recipe requirements?
- Can you develop processes to streamline cake production?
- Do you have experience creating uniform batches?
- Can you operate ovens simultaneously to meet required output and ensure baked products meet food safety and quality requirements?
- Are you able to analyze a product to determine the cause of unacceptable product quality?
- Do you have experience with cake decorating; chocolate tempering; preparing fillings; frosting/icing techniques?
- Are you familiar with estimating production needs based on demand?

Business

- Do you have experience balancing a register/terminal?
- Are you comfortable managing/counting cash, checks, and credit receipts in accordance with proper bookkeeping procedures?
- Do you have experience in processing sales; completing customer order forms, invoices and receipts; identifying and accurately processing customer delivery requirements?

- Do you have product development experience? Can you research opportunities for new products by identifying market characteristics and matching opportunities?
- Do you understand how to adapt an existing recipe to produce a new product, determine the method of assembly and presentation, and estimate the cost of production?
- Do you have experience managing a budget? Forecasting supply requirements?

Answering these questions is merely a guide to help you understand many of the roles most people don't consider when they think about starting a cake business. The questions also help identify skills in which you may require further experience. If you are confident in all but the business skills, then you are already on the right track by reading this book. There are also many good business, management, and accounting books on these topics. At the beginning stage, however, most entrepreneurs need the fundamentals. Much of the accounting, forecasting, budgeting, and inventory management can be learned relatively quickly and some of these responsibilities can be outsourced to professionals.

Of course, hiring someone to run the "business" part of your business is usually not an option. Your success depends on understanding the big picture. Too often, bakers, cake decorators, and hobbyists consider the artistry of the production the point at which their management ends. Unfortunately, these artists often end up losing sight of the financial condition of the business and eventually fail due to mismanagement. Moreover, as the leader, if you are making decisions based on guesswork, inaccurate assumptions and poor planning, then you will find it difficult to gain the confidence of those around you including staff, investors, and ultimately clients.

If you found most of your answers to be 'yes' for the business-related questions, but you don't have the cake skills, then you may need more experience baking and decorating cakes. Again, just as you can hire a professional to do any job, you are less likely to get the best from your employees if you are not an active participant or can't recognize errors. You need to understand how to make the product you will sell. It is human nature for an employee to have greater respect for someone who has mastered the task that they are being asked to carry out. More importantly, your business is a living entity that should change and grow over time. Your ability to duplicate any process -- whether a recipe or a sales technique -- depends on your ability to document and share it with your team.

Operations manual

Just as a good recipe needs to be written down in order to teach it to others efficiently, so too do the routines of running your business. A written record of every process in your business is key in teaching others the business so it can operate in your absence. An operations manual also helps you think concretely about each of the steps you must take on the daily, weekly, monthly, and annual basis. Many sample documents included in an operations manual can be found at our website:

http://cake-business.com/resources

Contact us if you have any trouble accessing these files by using the contact form on our website.

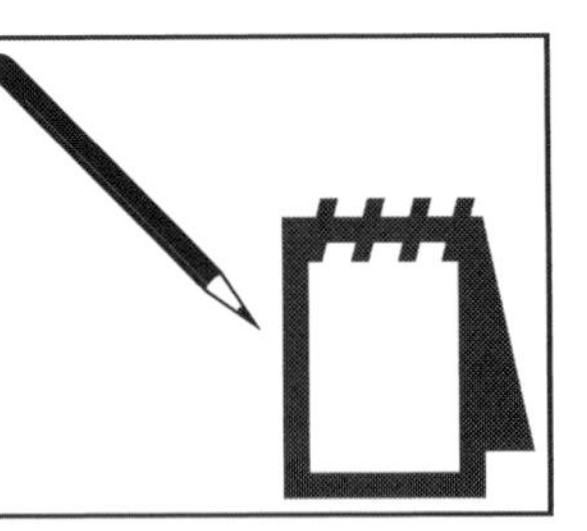

Get a job in a cake business/bakery

If you have the time, we strongly encourage you to get a job in the baking or hospitality industry (ideally a bakery that produces cakes and cupcakes). Be honest with your prospective employer about your ultimate objective to start a business. While some smaller shops may fear the appropriation of their recipes, most companies will recognize that everyone has to start somewhere and will appreciate your honesty. By working in a cake business you will learn if this is truly a good fit for you as well as the hard-won lessons of how a service business is run. Along the way, you will learn what to do, how to improve procedures, and become inspired for what your own cake business could be. Working in a bakery will teach you the day-to-day tasks, the stress of customer and financial demands, the interaction with customers, the business processes, and the lifestyle that you only gain on the job. However, without some previous kitchen experience, you will most likely find yourself in a role that has little to do with your ultimate objective, such as janitorial work.

Culinary school or on-the-job training

The choice to pursue formal education versus real-life experience is truly a personal one. A big part of the decision is your current skill level. Many of the professional schools assume a certain level of knowledge and emphasize advanced techniques, while a bakery owner will employ you as a dishwasher at first, even if you lack baking experience. Secondly, you must have a sense of what you ultimately want to get out of the time spent training yourself. Are you seeking a practical education, learned by working from the bottom up, or are you passionate about the fine details of the science, culture, and history of baked goods?

A hybrid of combining culinary school with on-the-job training may be the best approach. There is much to be learned and exposed to in both environments and each role enhances the other. Learning the techniques in an academic situation gives you the credibility to approach a bakery for the type of job you want. You can learn the best practices (both culinary and business) while applying that knowledge in a situation with real-world repercussions. The biggest drawback to pursuing a Culinary School Education is the cost. As an entrepreneur, you will need resources to start your bakery, and school can be very expensive.

A third option is to educate yourself by practicing every skill you want to master; reading books, networking with other bakers, and getting experience anywhere you can. This might include volunteering, working in a school kitchen, job shadowing, and working for family and friends. There are countless stories of food entrepreneurs who started by sharing their product with those around them, and then growing into full-fledged businesses. Your personal path has everything to do with your current experience and level of passion for filling in the gaps of your knowledge.

Desire and Inspiration

The most important traits of an entrepreneur are the ability to communicate your vision to others and make those people believers; the ability to balance the long-term vision with short-term survival; a refusal to listen to why your idea can't be done; and tenacity.

The next step I encourage new business owners to undertake is to think about their WHY. That is, why are you starting a cake business?

Whenever starting something unknown, time-consuming, or otherwise important, it helps to understand your WHY. Take 5-10 minutes now to write down and preserve your reasons for starting a cake business.

Knowing your WHY is an often-neglected first step in starting a business; yet, as you get going and challenges inevitably arise, you can always return to the foundation of your business, your WHY.

You may select this as the venture to undertake for several reasons. Perhaps you love baking, and over the years have become a pretty capable and creative baker. Do you have friends and family who say things like, "Your cakes are so good; you should go into business!"? Now is the time to transfer that talent into creating delicious treats for profit.

Perhaps you want to be able to schedule your own time and work at your convenience. For a small home-based operation, the baking and decorating of cakes can be done virtually at any time. You can do just about everything involved with the business within your home, except deliveries and trips to the market/bakery supply store.

Some entrepreneurs take action because of the lack of offerings in their community. They see a need and have a desire to fill it. For example, with the increased awareness and diagnosis of celiac disease, there is a greater demand for gluten-free baked goods. I know several people affected by this disease who have quit their jobs and started food businesses that provide high-quality products consumers want.

There are many reasons to start a business -- from wanting a better lifestyle for your family, to doing something positive for your neighbors. Take the time to write down your reasons now while you are thinking of it. It needn't be a lengthy document or polished for anyone else's reading. Just write freely whatever comes into your mind. The insight that you glean from this exercise may inform your mission statement or even the overall direction of your cake business. This writing exercise will also lead you to the next step on your path -- writing your business plan.

When thinking about your why, one way to get started is with a high level list of possible inspirations. Take a look at the list below to see if any of these phrases motivate you as a starting point for your why statement. If not, what other motivations do you have?

My motivation for starting a cake business is:

- Working from home
- I love the feeling of success when I share one of my cakes
- Supplementing my family income
- Making a lot of money
- A new show on the Food Network
- Being featured in Martha Stewart living
- I've dreamed of this since childhood
- I want a creative outlet
- There's nothing like this in our area
- I love running a business
- A shop in our town needs a new owner
- I want to be part of the larger community
- Other:

4
THE BUSINESS PLAN

Researching and writing your own business plan is an important step in starting your business. Regardless of whether you plan on operating a small cake business from your home, renting a commercial space, or opening a brick-and-mortar shop, writing a business plan is critical to your success. Not only will a business plan help you secure outside funding (should you seek it) and credit from suppliers, it will make you think through the tactical aspects of your business, exposing any holes that could ruin your business or cost you a lot of money.

This process is, for many people, where the fun, magical thinking of having a cake business meets the reality of how you will manage your day-to-day operation and finances; how you will promote and market your business; and the specific steps you will take to achieve your goals and objectives. Just as the art of making a beautiful cake requires recipes and preparation, the business requires a plan.

If you've never written a business plan, it might feel overwhelming at first. The key is to move through it one section at a time and seek assistance for the parts for which you don't have the expertise or information. Start with some of the easy parts first. If you get hung up on a particular part of the plan, skip it for now and come back and fill it in later. Don't worry about making a perfect first draft – just get some thoughts down to get the process going and you can always come back and polish it up later.

I am going to provide a high-level overview of what you can expect in each part and some of the research you will need to conduct as you work on your plan. Remember, you don't have to write a plan in any specific order and your local SCORE [http://www.score.org] or Small Business Administration (SBA) [www.sba.gov] office is happy to help you with your plan. SCORE and SBA provide free online and face-to-face business counseling, mentoring, and training. They helped me write my plan and they will help with yours.

Your business plan will consist of a narrative statement, an executive summary, and several financial worksheets. When creating your business plan, the executive summary, which appears at the beginning of the plan document, should actually be written last, as it is only *after* you've worked through the process of creating your plan that you can adequately summarize the details of your business.

It is a myth that if you are not seeking outside investment, you don't need a business plan. The real value of creating a business plan is not just in having the finished product in hand; rather, the value lies in the process of researching and thinking about your business in a systematic way. It takes you out of the daydream stage of thinking about recipes and happy customers, and requires you to think about what really matters--the sound operation of your business.

The act of planning forces you to conduct research and to look at your ideas critically. It takes time now, but avoids costly, perhaps disastrous, mistakes later. Ideally, you will discover both holes and opportunities in your current thinking. If you develop your numbers honestly and conservatively, the plan has the potential to highlight cash flow problems. Likewise, a thorough competitive analysis can show you how to capitalize on qualities that only you have and prepare for areas where you need help.

The business plan on our website is a hypothetical model, suitable as a guideline. However, you should modify it to suit your particular circumstances, whether you plan to be a small brick-and-mortar cake business, a home-based mail/web order shop, or a delivery-only start-up.

If you are creating a plan to show investors, pay particular attention to your writing style. You will be judged by the quality and appearance of your work as well as by your ideas. Keep in mind that the time most people will take to read your business plan is very limited. Your writing must be detailed enough to prove that you know what you're talking about, but succinct enough to get to the point quickly while you keep a reader's interest.

It typically takes several weeks to complete a good plan. Most of that time is not spent writing the plan, but conducting research and re-thinking your ideas and assumptions. But then, that's the value of the process, so make time to do the job properly. Along the way, be sure to keep detailed notes on your sources of information and on the assumptions underlying your financial data.

Before you start the plan, do some research in your community. Make sure you have considered the requirements for success:

Need – Does your community need the kind of cake business you want to create? The research indicates that the need is growing, but if there are already bakeries in your community, how can you profit from an underserved niche? What is unique about your cakes that would fill a need in your community? If there are many bakeries selling a comparable product line, would a different location be more competitive?

Customers – Are you thinking local or global? Are there enough potential local customers who will be interested in your cakes? If not, how will you reach the rest of the world? Will you sell online or try to market to retail operations like Whole Foods? If you are going local, how much will you have to spend on advertising to reach your potential clients? Can your community afford your ideal vision, or do you need to scale back? If you are going national, will you use a co-pack manufacturer or will you produce the cakes yourself?

Location – Will it be conveniently located? Can you afford the rent in a higher visibility area?

Products – Do you know what your prospective clients want? (An upscale, gourmet cake shop, a gluten-free alternative, etc.) Can you produce a product your customers want, at a price they want to pay and still make a profit? Remember that most successful cake shops are high volume businesses. You have to sell a large number of cakes to meet your financial goals each month. Fortunately, cakes are a low cost, low labor (usually), and high profit product.

Once you have answered the above success requirements, you will have a sense of the kind of thinking that goes into a business plan. The following chapter presents a high-level overview of what you can expect in each part and some of the research you will need to conduct as you develop your plan. Remember, you don't have to write a plan in any specific order and your local SCORE office is happy to help you. SCORE provides free online and face-to-face business counseling, mentoring, and training.

Elements of a Business Plan

A typical business plan has about 10 sections. Parts 1-4 describe your business and your product. Emphasize the elements of your cake business that will distinguish you from the competition and your particular skills and expertise. Talk about the market you are targeting and provide factual, non-hyped details for why this audience will buy from you. Explain what stage of development your business is in.

Section 1

1.1 Cover page

While seemingly obvious, a cover page is an important first impression that shows the reader, at a glance, the nature of the business and the professionalism of the author(s). Be sure to include the Business Name, your logo (if available), or a picture of your cakes and all of your contact information including your name, phone number, email address, and website (if complete).

1.2 Table of Contents

The Table of Contents is simply a list based on the headings of each section and subsection in the body of your document. This information is important because it gives a quick overview of the scope of the plan and enables readers to navigate quickly to specific areas of interest. A banker, for example, may skip past the narrative parts of the plan and go directly to the financials. An investor may only have an interest in the executive summary.

A Table of Contents can also be used to plan the document before you start writing. You can lay out the document in advance to build the skeleton of what you want the document to be. This does not mean you should complete the document in the order of the list or that the layout cannot change and grow. It is simply a good idea to know the framework of the business plan, rather than assembling something hodgepodge at the end.

1.3 Basic Information

You should provide a thorough list of the basics of your cake business -- The owners, partners, their addresses and contact information; business structure; professional advisers such as accountant, attorney, and banking contacts.

1.4 Introduction

This is a brief narrative that introduces the business to which the rest of the plan refers. The intro should explain the purpose of the plan as a planning tool and fund raising vehicle. Briefly introduce the author and the layout of the plan.

2. Summary

A summary highlights the key points you want readers to take away. If a reader only has time to read a single page of your plan, imagine the importance of this section. The summary should comprise your complete business on a single page of 4-5 paragraphs. It is written after the plan has been drafted because you don't know what to summarize until you have written it. This section should be succinct -- about two pages or 10% of the total plan in length. Additionally it should paint a positive, yet realistic picture. For some readers the summary is the sales pitch and will determine if further reading is of interest. Be sure to give this section plenty of time.

3. Business Description

While it might seem obvious to you, explain what business you will be in and what you will sell. Begin with a general description in a single sentence such as: "Gourmet, vegan cakes made from the finest locally-sourced ingredients."

You might include:

3.1 A Mission Statement

Do you offer something unique and consider it your mission to bring it to market? (e.g. organic or gluten-free) Take a moment now to write down a draft of your mission statement, which is a concise paragraph describing what your company does and for whom. It is the essence of your brand.

Example Mission Statement from Best Maid Cake Company:

"We strive to be a company where genuine commitment to quality is clearly shown in our product, our work environment, and our customer. Since 1943, our family values of honesty, integrity, and trust have been the cornerstone of our business that we extend to our employees, our customers, and our community."

A mission statement needs to be simple and brief enough that anyone reading it quickly understands your company's most basic goals -- your mission. Over time, as you work on setting up your business, you may want to return to your mission statement and revise or fine-tune it.

In addition to writing your mission statement, you should also take the time to write your WHY statement, as discussed in Chapter 3.

3.2 Company Goals and Objectives

Explain why you want to be in the cake business. This statement should reflect the underlying reasons for starting and running your cake business. These objectives could cover growth, profitability, offerings, and markets. For example, an objective could be profitability within 2 years. Objectives are shorter-term markers along the way to goal achievement. A goal might be a successful franchise operation of your initial cake concept in 5 years, or opening a retail location if you are a home business. The objectives might be annual sales targets and some specific measures of customer satisfaction. Setting goals may seem like forecasting and vague estimation. However, if you don't set objectives and goals, you will be running your cake business hoping that at the end of the month/year, you will be taking in more money than you are paying out. This approach will almost always bring failure. Measurable goals and objectives show you, before it's too late, how well (or poorly) you are doing.

3.3 Business Philosophy

What is important to you about running a cake business? There is a reason you are reading this book-- a desire and ultimate purpose. Documenting your own personal philosophy will help sell your business to others. This statement is closely related to your WHY statement from the previous chapter, but this one is public, whereas your WHY is personal. You may find that your business philosophy and your WHY are identical, but they don't have to be.

3.4 Overview of Your Market and the Cake/Bakery Industry.

What changes are on the horizon (long-term and short-term) for small food producers? How do you plan to prepare and capitalize on them? For example, we've seen a huge growth in organic, vegan, and restrictive diet products in the last few years. There are always new innovations in production techniques. Perhaps new government regulations could impact your cake business. This section of your business plan should identify any change that could positively or negatively affect your business.

3.5 Strengths and Core Competencies

What factors will make your cake business succeed? What do you think your major competitive strengths will be? Examples: Do you have a recipe that is already famous in your town? Is there a large audience, such as a college campus, that needs a cake delivery business? What background experience, skills, and strengths do you personally bring to this new venture?

3.6 Legal Form of Ownership

This section explains the legal status of your company. Sole Proprietor, Partnership, Corporation, Limited Liability Corporation (LLC) and why you have selected this form (See the chapter, Legal Considerations).

4. Products and Services

In this section, you will describe your cakes. You can list the individual recipes you sell or you might describe the pricing structure of the different sizes or combinations such as cake bouquets or gift baskets. You might also provide a general pricing structure for wholesale vs. retail sales. This is a great opportunity to think about pricing.

Basic questions to consider:

- What position or image do you want to convey?
- What sets your cakes, as well as your customer service, above your competition?
- How broad will your cake product line be?
- What new products or services will you introduce over time?
- What brand concept will you try to develop or reinforce? (All-natural, extravagant, old-fashioned, etc.)
- What will be your pricing strategies? (For example: premium, indulgent, local)
- Why will customers pay your price?
- What will your credit policies be for wholesale/retail clients?

4.1 Pricing

Outline your proposed pricing plan for each cake variation (e.g. individual, dozen, bulk, minimum orders, wedding favors, catering, etc.) If you plan to do catering or bulk orders, think about the different types of pricing models. Use simple tables and put any detailed pricelist or menu in the appendix.

4.2 Competitive Analysis

Which cake shops, bakeries, and other businesses/products compete with you?

First, identify how many bakeries selling handmade cakes are in your market area. Then, identify those that appeal to the types of customers that you plan to serve. You should also identify all other bakeries located in your immediate area, even if they don't sell cakes, because they can also influence your business. Consider including grocery stores, farmer's markets, delis, etc. Refer to the Yellow Pages, or websites like Yelp.com for listings of area bakeries that sell comparable treats.

It is important to identify any bakeries, especially cake-selling shops, that have closed, and for what reasons. Also, learn what new bakeries, sweet-shops, delis, etc. are planned in your proposed community and determine how they might affect your operation. If you plan to sell online, identify those cake businesses as well as mail-order companies.

After identifying your competition, visit and evaluate the ones (at least two) that you sense will be your greatest competition. Speak with the manager of these operations if possible. Use the following checklist to take notes for your analysis. (If you are a home-based operation this process might be limited to other cake businesses selling in competing venues such as farmer's markets or selling wholesale.)

Location

- Community traffic patterns
- Proximity to sources of demand
- Accessibility
- Visibility
- Surrounding neighborhood
- Parking availability
- Sign visibility

Appearance/Comfort

- Exterior appearance and theme
- Interior appearance and theme

- Atmosphere
- Cleanliness
- Heating and ventilation

Menu

- Theme
- Variety and selection
- Signature items
- Price range and value
- Beverage choices

Quality

- Taste
- Presentation
- Portion size
- Consistency

Service

- Days open
- Hours of operation
- Service style

Quality of Service

- Speed of Service
- Friendliness

General Information

- Number of seats
- Types of guests served (age, income, origin, etc.)
- Is business expanding or reducing staff?
- Catering?
- Entertainment
- Franchise affiliation
- Reviews by food Critics/Ratings in travel guides, Yelp

- Local reputation
- Advertising and promotion methods used website quality

Overall

- Strengths
- Weaknesses

With your notes, create a competitive analysis comparison table. This table will include columns for each of your competitors, yourself, and the above competitive factors. You will rate your competitors and yourself from 1 to 5 (1 = weak; 5 = strong). Try to be very honest here. A competitive analysis can be very informative. You should discover areas in which you are weak and areas in which you can capitalize on the failings of your competitors. And remember, you cannot be all things to all people.

In the final column, estimate the importance of each competitive factor to the customer: 5 = critical; 1 = not very important. Use this number to weigh the scores more accurately by multiplying it by the individual scores. Scoring higher on the factors that customers most care about obviously outweighs poor scores on the less critical factors.

Don't skip this step! Even if you don't include it in the business plan, a competitive analysis can inform everything from your menu to your advertising. See the Small Business Administration for more guidance:

http://1.usa.gov/OpaK1q

After completing the graph, write a short paragraph stating your competitive advantages and disadvantages. Understanding your strengths and weaknesses will help you carve out your niche and your strategy.

Remember that you cannot be all things to all people. In fact, trying to be causes the customer to have difficulty understanding how you fit in their shopping universe. You want the target customer to think of you in a very specific way so that your business comes to mind when they are thinking about purchasing a cake. What do you want your customers to think of when they think of your cake business?

5. Customer Profile

This is a very important, though sometimes ignored or avoided, section. Allow plenty of space to identify your targeted customers, their characteristics, and their geographic locations (otherwise known as their demographics). While this data can be very challenging for a start-up cake business owner to acquire, it is important that the research be clear, specific, and authentic. This information will convey if there really is a sustainable demand. If you plan on wholesale clients in addition to your retail operation, you should also analyze this demographic.

You may have more than one customer group. Identify the most important ones. For example, you may want to consider the difference between the customers who buy from you during the weekday, and those who shop on weekends. If you have a farmer's market presence, then think about the difference for each customer group and construct a demographic profile. Do this for each major group of customers. Include the following:

- Age
- Gender
- Location
- Income level
- Social class and occupation
- Education
- Other (specific to your industry)

For wholesale business customers, the demographic factors might be:

- Industry (such as restaurant or caterer)
- Location
- Size of business and buying potential
- Price and product preferences

One way to convey the potential value for wholesale clients, such as restaurants, is to quantify these customers within your community and estimate the value of their business. For example, if there are 100 restaurants in your surrounding region, what is the most likely number that will do business with you? What is the theoretical value of a single contract (e.g. 3 dessert cakes per week) over a year? What is the growth potential as you ramp up your operation and can meet more business demand? You may find that wholesale margins are too slim compared to selling directly to your own customers until you have greater scale.

There are two kinds of market research: primary and secondary. Primary research involves gathering your own data. For example, you could use the yellow pages to identify competitors, and do surveys or focus-group interviews to learn about consumer preferences. A traffic count is another data point you can research yourself if you are opening a retail operation. You simply go to the location you're considering and count the cars that pass. Typically, you count the cars that pass on the same side as the location for an hour in the morning, at noon, and during evening rush hour. Average the traffic to approximate the daily numbers. How about foot traffic? Often the local Chamber of Commerce, or even the landlord, will have these numbers. Professional market research can be very costly, but there are many books that show small business owners how to conduct effective research themselves.

Secondary research means using published information such as industry profiles, trade journals, newspapers, magazines, census data, and demographic profiles. This type of information is available in public libraries, industry associations, Chambers of Commerce, from vendors who sell to your industry, and from government agencies. ZipSkinny [zipskinny.com] and FedStats [fedstats.gov] can provide some initial demographic information. Demographic maps can also be purchased. [buydemographics.com] These maps provide detailed population estimates, the current and predicted number of households, families, median age, and median household income. These numbers will help you project the size and income of your target audience. You should also consider purchasing a "Retail Goods and Services Expenditures" map for your community, as this will tell you how much people in your proposed location spend on bakery goods in a year. Obviously, it is advantageous to locate a cake shop in an area where household income and food expenditure is higher. These maps are eye-opening and well worth the minimal investment.

Start with your local library. Most librarians are pleased to guide you through their business data collection. You will be amazed at what is there. There are more online sources than you could possibly use. Your Chamber of Commerce also has good information on the local area. Bakery trade associations and trade publications often have excellent data geared toward the bakery industry in general. You will have to make some assumptions for cake-specific business information.

In your marketing plan, be as specific as possible; give statistics, numbers, and sources. The marketing plan will be the basis, later on, of the all-important sales projection. Most importantly, remember that conducting research involves more than sitting behind your computer. This step requires you to go out into the world, look around your community, talk to others, and gather information.

If you are a home-based operation, you should still conduct market research. While you may not need traffic patterns or complex financial analyses, you need to document your assumptions about who will buy your cakes.

6. Marketing, Sales and Projections

No matter how good your cakes are, your business cannot succeed without effective marketing. You should have already uncovered a lot of information about your target market.

Use the business planning process as your opportunity to consider the best ways to reach them. Indicate specific tactics you will use to bring customers to you.

If you are selling online, what methods will you use to advertise your cake business? Facebook? Twitter? Have you identified low-cost methods to get the most out of your promotional budget?

Will you use methods other than paid advertising, such as word-of-mouth (How will you stimulate it?), free press, and social networking?

What image do you want to project? How do you want customers to see you? In addition to advertising, what plans do you have for graphic image support? This includes logo design, cards and letterhead, brochures, signage, and interior design (if customers come to your place of business).

Should you have a system to identify repeat customers and then systematically contact them on Facebook and Twitter? I have an annual schedule -- completely automated using email -- for reaching out to my prospective customers. Services such as Constant Contact, Mailchimp, Get Response, and aweber.com make it easy to follow up with your customers and fans for easy repeat business.

Promotional Budget

How much will you spend on the items listed above? What is the promotion strategy before start-up? (These numbers will go into your start-up budget.) How much will you spend on marketing monthly? (These numbers will go into your operating plan budget.)

7. Management Team

It is important for anyone reading your business plan to know your qualifications, as well as the structure of your new business. If you do not have extensive business experiences, do not inflate this area. Rather, be honest about your background and focus on your passion for baking cakes. More importantly, if your plan reflects a lack of business experience, then you should seek trusted advisors who can guide you. This may be a relative or friend who may be an unpaid consultant. The main thing is to have someone you can contact when you have questions.

8. Operations

This section describes how you will produce your cakes. You should include details that estimate the production process timeline and quantity of goods you will make each day. Any key supplier relationships, such as bulk ingredients or paper goods supplier, should be identified here.

Questions to consider:

- How and where are your cakes produced?
- How will you get your items to wholesale vendors? If you are selling online, how will you ship? How will you keep products fresh?
- What is the capacity of your baking set-up and can you produce enough cakes to meet sales goals?
- Do you have any specialized production techniques or recipes? If so, are there any associated costs?
- How will you insure quality control?
- What is your customer service policy/approach?
- How much raw ingredient inventory will you keep?
- How will you manage it?
- What qualities do you need in a location? Describe the type of location you'll have. If you are running a home cake business, are there limitations of using a consumer kitchen that will impact you?

Physical Requirements

- Amount (sq. footage) of space: Include a floor plan if possible to the addendum.
- Type of building
- Zoning. Confirm that your proposed location is properly zoned.
- Power and other utilities. Does the current configuration meet your needs?

Cost

Estimate your occupation expenses, including rent, but also include maintenance, utilities, insurance, and initial remodeling costs to make the space suit your needs. These numbers will become part of your financial plan. What will be your business hours?

8.1 Legal Environment

Describe the following:

- Licensing and inspection requirements
- Permits
- Health, workplace, environmental regulations

- Zoning or building code requirements
- Insurance coverage

8.2 Suppliers

Identify key suppliers:

- Names and addresses
- Type and amount of inventory furnished
- Credit and delivery policies
- History and reliability

Should you have more than one supplier for critical items (as a backup)? Are there occasions or times of the year, such as the holidays, where shortages could be a problem? Are the costs of basic ingredients, such as eggs, flour, chocolate, etc., steady or fluctuating? If suddenly any one of your primary cake ingredients was in shortage, how would you deal with changing costs?

9. Personnel

The success of many small bakeries depends on their ability to recruit, train, and retain employees. Given that many cake businesses and bakeries are small operations at first, this area may not have much emphasis. However, it should not be ignored, as readers of your plan will want to know you are thinking about the future. Even if you are a one-person operation now, at some point if your business grows, you will need employees.

10. References

Here, you identify your professional service providers including your accountant, insurance agent, lawyer, and your local bank manager. It is also beneficial to list any professional consultants or advisors familiar with your business. Don't worry if you don't have each of these relationships figured out yet. Come back to this (and every) section as you make final decisions.

Questions to consider:

- What are staffing needs now? In the future?
- What skills must they have? What training will you provide?
- Are the people you need available?
- What is their compensation?

11. Financial Projections

You must create some financial projections that will give you, and anyone looking at your plan, a snapshot of the future financial health of your business. This may seem impossible if you don't have any previous records of what to expect. That is why it is so important! You must thoughtfully and honestly assess future cash flows.

Part of your business plan will include the financial numbers you already have and/or the forecasts for the future. You will undertake some research for this part. You will include the following:

- Sales Forecast and Strategy
- (Projected) Pro Forma Income Statement
- Break-even Analysis
- Projected Cash Flow
- Projected Balance Sheet

Forecasting helps you allocate your resources (including start-up cash), handle unforeseen complications, and make good business decisions. Because it provides specific and organized information about your cake business and how you will repay borrowed money, a good business plan is a crucial part of any loan application. Additionally, it informs suppliers and others about your requirements and goals. Finally, beyond the descriptions you provide, the financial data will help prove the viability of your cake business. You have to make the numbers work to show that what you are planning will, in time, break even and profit. For example, some people begin broadly by estimating the goals they hope to achieve in order to maintain a certain lifestyle and pay off a loan. Others start with the goal of breaking even and plan for increased profits over time.

Often, a new entrepreneur will have a vision for a cake business and then find a location or commercial kitchen for rent. Armed with the monthly rent as a baseline expense, she will then start her research for all of the other expenses such as utilities, insurance, build-out costs, equipment, ingredients, etc. While this is important data, it is critical to look at the sales strategy and revenue projections that you can realistically expect from your community.

The financial aspect of starting a business, for most people, is very complicated and therefore avoided. Unfortunately, this leads to magical thinking about money -- the ideal dream that you will concentrate on making great cakes and that so much money will come in, that cash flow won't be a problem for you. This rarely (if ever) holds true, so it is important to understand the basics of cash flow.

The budgets and financial projections of your business plan will convey to potential investors that you not only understand, but also are planning for paying your bills and driving your business toward profitability. It will also provide a realistic baseline of what to expect for your personal finances. This section should be completed honestly and conservatively, as experienced business people will be examining these numbers carefully. A complete set of spreadsheets and worksheets is provided on our website to help you.

Sales Forecast and Strategy

For your business plan to be convincing, you have to provide a realistic sales forecast. In fact, this forecast is the single most critical piece of information in the plan because it indicates the likelihood for success. Moreover, the sales forecast is used in other areas of the plan, such as cash flow projections and budgets. For example, if you think you will sell more than 10 cakes per week, you might need a far different oven, staff, marketing plan and inventory setup than if you estimated 1-3 cakes per week as a home bakery. How many cakes per week are realistic for the kind of business you're planning? Will you sell other baked goods such as cupcakes or cake balls? Are you planning a smaller or larger business?

Of course, you have to have the strategy in place to reach those numbers; the cash flow to meet the expenses; the infrastructure to make and sell the quantity that will make you profitable; the customer base desiring your product. Forecasting is kind of like juggling all of those different requirements and assumptions at once. You will find yourself playing with the numbers to the point where the goals seem achievable and the revenue acceptable. If the data point to a satisfactory profit that fits with your personal financial situation and repays any outside investors, then the business plan is working.

Unfortunately, if you don't have any previous sales data to rely on, it is much more difficult to estimate how many cakes you will sell each month. An informed, legitimate sales forecast can be created from some assumptions about: the market in which your cake business will operate; the competition; the wedding and bakery trends seen in comparable communities; the spending patterns locally. One way to ensure your estimates are accurate, and perceived as credible, is to provide documentation and back-up your numbers with hard data. In other words, you have to write up a justification for the sales figures that draws on real data, not just guesswork.

One way to determine sales in your community is to network with bakeries in comparable communities (as they are not in competition with you). You can often find sales figures online for bakeries that are for sale, or have closed and use those numbers to extrapolate your own figures as a starting point. (Bizbuysell.com is a good place to find bakeries for sale.) Another technique is to estimate sales potential of a geographic target area based on the target customer you are after. For example, how many weddings take place in your community each year and what is the typical budget? Talk with potential customers about their wedding plans or with recent brides about their wedding cake purchase. If you are focusing more on celebration cakes, conduct interviews with the moms in your circle of friends, as they are the most common cake buyers.

Your customer profile research from Section Five will provide the demographic data (population estimates, the current and predicted number of households, families, median age, and median household income) and can help you estimate the size of the marketplace. If you look at the size of the customer base and their consumption habits you can also make some estimations on what percentage of those customers will buy from you. The investment in professional demographic maps is well worth it.

You can also conduct some very simple and useful test marketing at farmer's markets with little expense and no risk. While it can be frustrating to delay the launch of your business to conduct preliminary research, it is wise to start slowly with realistic sales expectations and ensure the business is feasible.

Finally, if you have difficulty obtaining sales figures directly, you can try several secondary sources of information. Many suppliers have very sophisticated computer modeling to estimate how much inventory a food business of your proposed scale would require. They can help estimate your market based on what they are providing other bakeries. You might also try to talk to former employees of the competition or closed businesses. Of course, the national trade associations will have some guidelines to share with you as a member. Finally, you can hire an experienced consultant to help set realistic goals.

Table 1 shows a hypothetical sales forecast for a wedding cake and cupcake business. The forecast assumes 1-2 cakes per/week for a spring, summer, and autumn wedding season, and a robust cupcake business that might include weddings, parties, and wholesale accounts.

Unit Sales

Your sales projections will be your best guess based on your research as discussed above. You can do this projection multiple times with different scenarios such as best-case, worst-case, etc., based on your understanding of the economic climate, the perceived demand in your community, and your competition.

Sales Revenue

Sales Revenue is the total unit sales times the prices for each unit. In the example below, the total unit sale of cupcakes, multiplied by the price per cupcake ($3.00) is $21,150.

Direct Unit Price or COGS (cost of goods sold)

The cost of goods sold will be determined by costing your recipes and using a cake pricing matrix (see resources on our website: cake-business.com/resources). Cake units are measured in servings. Because cake pricing is a variable that depends upon servings and customization, the unit is averaged in the table below.

Table 1

Sales Forecast	
Unit Sales	
Cake Servings	6240
Cupcakes	7050
Total Unit Sales	**13290**
Direct Unit Prices	
Cakes (average price per serving)	$2.53
Cupcakes	$3.00
Sales Revenue	
Cakes	$15,787
Cupcakes	$21,150
Total Sales Revenue	$36937
Direct Cost of Sales	
Cakes	$2076
Cupcakes	$4089
Subtotal Direct Costs of Sales	**$6165**

Table 1: Sample Sales Forecast Cake Servings and Cupcakes

Once you have an estimate of sales, you can begin to articulate some other parts of the plan and make some high level assumptions about expenses and profits.

Start-Up Budget

You will have many expenses before you even begin operating your business. The start-up budget is used to determine how much money will be needed to start your cake business and keep it operating until you make a profit. Since businesses do not always make a profit the first year (or more), cash is needed to keep the operation going until enough money is generated to cover all the expenses. The start-up budget can be used to determine how much money you will need to start your business.

It's important to estimate these expenses accurately, and then to plan where you will get sufficient capital. Most business owners who open retail operations will tell you that arriving at the time where the first cake could be sold was much more costly than they anticipated. There are two ways to make allowances for surprise expenses. The first is to overestimate the actual cost of each item in the budget. The problem with that approach, however, is that it destroys the accuracy of your carefully researched numbers. The best approach is to add a separate line item, called "contingencies," to account for the unforeseeable expenses such as a broken air conditioner, a donation to the local street festival, a new grease trap, etc. A rule of thumb is that contingencies should equal at least 20% of the total of all other start-up expenses.

What are my start-up costs?

To start a brick-and-mortar cake business, you need to have first and foremost, a location, equipment and furnishings, utilities (electricity, water, HVAC), someone to do the work (you), and products to sell.

Start-up costs also include installation of fixtures and equipment, deposits for public utilities, licenses and permits, accounting and legal services, and business insurance. A special start-up cost is the start-up inventory. This is the dollar amount for the raw ingredients you purchase to sell to your customers as cakes and it is an ongoing expense.

To equip a retail cake bakery completely, the purchase of furnishings for the entryway, restrooms, dining room (if applicable), kitchen, storage, office, and employee areas must be included. The concept (design, brand, and theme) should be carried through in everything you do.

Table 2 shows the typical start-up costs for a shop with dining space (Ex.2), compared to a home cake business (Ex.1). These numbers are hypothetical because much of your business expense depends on the scale of your business and your sales goals. The operating expenses projected for the first three months of operation are listed as "Suggested Operating Capital," which means the amount of cash you will need in addition to the start-up funds to run the business for three months. Ideally, you should have enough cash for six months, taking into account contingencies such as slower times of the year.

Table 2

Item	Ex. 1	Ex. 2
Rent (Sec. Deposit & 1st month)	0	10,000
Initial Inventory/Ingredients	2,000	11,000
Equipment/Fixtures	0	50,000
Improvements and Build-out	0	18,500
Licenses, Tax Deposits and Permits	300	500
Utilities Deposit	0	300
Employees	0	7,500
Grand Opening Advertising	0	3,000
Legal Services	150	800
Accounting	100	1,000
Insurance	1,000	3,000
Loan Fees	0	2,000
Incorporation	100	500
Signage	0	10,000
Misc.	500	1,000
Total Costs	4150	119,100
Suggested Operating Capital	3000	40,000
Total	7150	**159,100**

Table 2: Cake Business Start-Up Budget

Use this chart as a guide for your own budget and keep in mind that rent, legal and professional fees, marketing costs, etc, are greatly dependent upon the location of your business. These figures are illustrative of how to create your budget, not representative of any one business. That said, notice that Example 1 has no money allocated for build out, utilities, employees, etc. This is a home-business example. The primary expenses might include a second fridge, mixer, and an initial order of ingredients and supplies. Example 2 shows a retail cake shop in a high-traffic urban center. Your task is to apply the general categories to your own situation. These numbers must be realistic and documented. You can look online for equipment costs, call prospective service providers, and use online forums to talk to other business owners about many of these estimates.

One technique for discerning prices in your area is to talk to non-competitive parallel business, such as a bread bakery or ice-cream shop. They can give you advice without feeling like they are aiding their competition.

When you start finalizing your estimates, be sure to keep a log of how you came up with the number (a simple notebook or spreadsheet will do). If the data points are particularly relevant or unique, you can include them in an appendix.

Operating Budget

Similar in format to the start-up budget above, the operating budget is a spending plan for all of the things you will need to run your cake business. The difference is that the analysis is for 3, 6, or 12 months, made up of the ongoing expenses. The budget lists the type of expense and corresponding amount that will be paid on a monthly basis to keep the business operating.

Typical ongoing operating expenses include:

- Advertising
- Insurance/Utilities
- Health Insurance
- Loan Repayment (amount of interest and capital required to repay the loan each month). Indicate the terms of the loan.
- Taxes
- Payroll
- Payroll Tax Expenses
- Medicare Tax Expense
- Social Security Tax Expense
- Rent
- Workman's Compensation Insurance
- Supplies
- Telephone
- Water
- COGS (Cost of Goods Sold)
- Maintenance/Repairs of Equipment
- Accounting/Legal/Depreciation

Pro Forma Income Statement

A pro forma income statement is a look at revenue and expense projections for future periods. Based on your market research and a few assumptions, the pro forma statement will help you organize, evaluate, and quantify the results. The pro forma income statement will also help you form an idea of what it will take to make a profit and be successful. This document is important in a business plan because it communicates the economic viability of your cake business. The example in Table 3 shows one year. Although some bankers and investors require one-, three-, or five-year estimates, a single year is usually sufficient in constructing a pro forma income statement. The pro forma income statement does not arrive at the true net income (or loss) for your bakery because variables such as depreciation, income taxes, interest, and utility hookups are not easily estimated.

The first item is the Projected Revenue. You should have already calculated this in the Sales Forecast (Table 1). Likewise, you will pull the Unit Sales and COGS from your sales forecast (Table 1). Your Expenses will be determined by your research and estimations from the Operating Budget. Chapters 10 and 11 will address, in greater detail, the expenses you will encounter and will assist you in compiling accurate estimations.

When everything is added up, the result is a one-year analysis. Your profit projections should be accompanied by a paragraph or two explaining how you estimated your income and expenses. Keep careful notes on your research and assumptions, so that you can explain them later, if necessary, and also so that you can refer to your sources when it's time to revise your plan.

Table 3

Annual Gross Profit		**Totals**
Projected sales		**$100,000**
Less Direct Costs		
Raw Ingredients	$10,000	
Sub-Contractors	$10,000	
Direct Labor	$25,000	
Total Direct Costs		**$45,000**

Gross Profit		**$55,000**
<u>Gross Profit Margin</u>		
Gross Profit	$55,000	
Sales	$100,000	
Gross Profit Margin		**55.0%**
<u>Overhead</u>		
Audit / Accounting Fees	$100	
Bus Dev. - Travel	$250	
Bus. Dev. - Entertainment	$500	
Bus. Dev. - Meals	$500	
Capital Acquisitions	n/a	
Charitable Contributions	$100	
Commissions	$250	
Conferences and Seminars	$100	
Consulting Fees	$0	
Depreciation	$250	
Employee Benefits	$0	
Entertainment	$150	
Equipment Lease	$100	
Facilities - Insurance	$100	
Facilities - Phone	$500	
Facilities - Property Taxes	$0	
Facilities - Rent	$0	
Facilities - Security	$0	
Facilities - Utilities	$250	
Facility - Other	$0	
Financial Charges	$0	

Furniture	$150	
Insurance	$250	
Inventory Purchases	n/a	
IT Consulting	$0	
Legal Fees	$100	
Loan Capital	n/a	
Loan Interest	$0	
Miscellaneous	$500	
Office Supplies	$250	
Payroll - Operational Staff	n/a	
Payroll - Administrative Staff	$0	
Payroll - Owner / Directors	$0	
Payroll - Sales / Marketing	$0	
Payroll Taxes	$0	
Postal / Shipping	$500	
PR / Advertising	$500	
Repairs and Maintenance	$250	
Research and Development	$0	
Storage	$0	
Subscriptions and Dues	$100	
Taxes and Licenses	$500	
Telecommunications	$100	
Vehicle Expenses	$250	
Overhead		$6,600
Break-Even Point (Annual)		
Overheads	$6,600	
Gross Profit Margin	55.0%	
Break-Even Point		**$12,000**
Break-Even Point (Monthly)		

Overhead	$6,600	
Gross Profit Margin	55.0%	
Break-Even Point		**$1,000**
Estimated Profit		
Projected Annual Sales	$100,000	
Break-Even Sales	$12,000	
	$88,000	
Gross Profit Margin	55.0%	
Estimated Profit		**$48,400**

Table 3: Pro Forma Income Statement (Add the Date And Year)

Note: the figures used in this table are not representative of a working cake business. Rather, they are simple numbers to illustrate the breakdown of data. A template is provided on cake-business.com for you to provide your actual numbers.

Break-Even Analysis

A break-even analysis predicts the sales volume (the quantity of cake servings), at a given price, required to recover total costs. Simply stated, a break-even analysis helps you determine if you can make enough money each month to cover your expenses at the prices you set for your goods. You need to bring your best estimations to this process and understand some basic concepts. A break-even analysis is included in most business plans because it shows at a very high level, the initial goals the entrepreneur must set. While there are mathematical formulas used to calculate the break-even analysis, the easiest method is to use a web-based break-even calculator.

Web Resource: http://tinyurl.com/breakev

Use this online calculator to help determine your break-even point, the amount of revenue you need to generate to cover your monthly costs.

To determine if your cake business will be viable, you must first estimate how much revenue you will bring in each month with a sales forecast. (See Table 1.) While the estimates generated by your own research are a great starting point, you should rely on a good local accountant with food service experience, or someone who understands the restaurant or bakery business to confirm your numbers. This is especially true if you are going to invest in a retail space.

When calculating your break-even point, you need to know a few additional data variables. The first element is the unit cost per item (or cost of goods sold) that you sell. For a cake business, this is cost per serving. In order to calculate your cost per serving, you first figure out how much a single recipe (cake, buttercream or fondant, torte) costs to make. This is called "costing your recipes" down to the penny.

The first step in recipe costing is adding up the cost of the ingredients used. Since you may be purchasing items in bulk, you should calculate the price for a single unit of weight (grams or kilograms) for the entire bag, bottle, carton, etc., of each ingredient. In other words, if you buy a 50 pound bag of flour, the first step is to convert it to kilograms, then calculate the cost of each kilogram.

Here's an example. Say the price of flour in bulk is $21.59 for a 50-pound or 22.7 kilogram bag; thus, the cost is $0.95 per kilograms (21.59 ÷ 22.7). With that rate, convert your recipes to kilograms and determine how much of each ingredient is used to make a batch.

Once you know the base unit price of a kilogram of flour, sugar, baking soda, etc., you can convert your recipe into kilograms. For example, if your recipe calls for 2 3/4 cups of all-purpose flour, it will convert to 0.34 kg. The total cost of flour used in this recipe is $0.14.

Table 4

	Ingredient	Price /kg	Cost/ingredient in recipe
1	All Purpose Flour	0.4150	0.14
2	Champagne	6.0215	1.20
3	Salt	0.9362	0.00
4	Baking Powder	3.0047	0.03
5	Butter	6.6225	1.50
6	Sugar	0.7906	0.15
7	Egg White	2.6687	0.67
		Batch Cost	3.70

Table 4: Recipe Costing

The recipe yields 4.5 cups of batter, or about 12.5 servings of cake. Dividing the total cost of all the ingredients by the number of servings will provide you with the total cost per serving (about $0.30). Of course, this accounts for only one layer and no frosting. You can complete this process manually for each recipe you use in a cake. Additionally, you would add in extra costs for fillings, decorations, fondant, your time, etc. The economies of scale will lower the total cost per serving.

Don't worry if this seems too difficult. In the resources section of our website, we provide a handy cake pricing matrix for doing these calculations. Once you know how much a single serving of cake costs to make, you have a much greater appreciation for maximizing the efficiency of your operation, keeping a keen eye on your supplies and suppliers, and most importantly, setting your prices for profit.

This first calculation is known in accounting terms as the Costs of Goods Sold (or COGS). Use a pricing matrix to determine your price per serving. Here's an example: You sell a cake that serves 116 (with a top layer of 14) for $344.55. The total cost of ingredients and supplies is $58 using the recipe above. Factoring in your hourly rate, your total profit is $156 or $1.20 per serving. Note: These calculations are for illustrative purposes only, using the most basic/ economical cake design. A more complex cake can yield a higher profit margin. How many cake servings (cupcakes, cake balls, etc) do you need to sell each month to pay your bills? This is known as your break-even point.

In order to figure your break-even point, you need your estimated running costs. This includes your payroll, rent, loan payment, utilities, etc. Let's assume you have $1,000 in expenses each month. Use the worksheet provided on our website to estimate your expenses. Do not include the cost to make the cake (COGS).

Using the break-even formula (Break-Even Point = Fixed Costs) (Unit Selling Price - Variable Costs), or more simply a break-even calculator, your cake business would need $1,600 in revenue to meet all of the $1,000 in expenses. If you only sold (the most basic, no-frills) cake and no other products, you would have to sell 1,333 servings per month, or 10 (130 serving) cakes.

To save time converting your non-metric weights, use a specialized cooking conversion calculator: Web Resource: http://tinyurl.com/cakecalc

If you are not familiar with measuring your recipes by weight, you should learn this process. Measuring by weight has many advantages including:

- **Greater Accuracy**: Weight is more accurate than volume, since it isn't affected by how well packed or sifted, finely or coarsely chopped, etc. the ingredient is.
- **Simplicity**: It's quicker and simpler. By measuring directly into the mixing bowl, there are no measuring cups to level off, no messes from leveling off measuring cups, less need for sifting, and no dirty measuring cups to wash.
- **Commercial Recipes**: Recipes can specify any weight, without being restricted to the specific sizes of measuring cups available. There is no more need for oddball measures like "one cup minus two tablespoons" as is seen in some recipes. Note, a good scale that measures in grams and/or kilograms will also save a great deal of time.

If you estimate your daily process, such as when you start baking in the morning, how many batches you can make with the number of ovens you plan to have, the time required making sales and running the business, etc., you should be able to estimate the output of a single person. Your numbers should reflect realistic assumptions. If your operation requires higher output, that means additional staff and additional costs.

In order to be profitable, you have to be efficient. This means having a product mix that is easy to create and sells well. When choosing recipes, you may be tempted to start with extravagant recipes. Be advised that most brides prefer either chocolate, white cake, or spice/carrot cake. (Lemon is also popular in the summer.)

Build your business around a few simple recipes, as they will account for a huge percentage of your orders. Add other recipes when and if the demand exists. The three basic recipes to consider using should include very simple ingredients and be quick and easy to prepare. Find cakes that are low-labor and high-profit: dump, mix, bake, and decorate. You might couple this menu with a specialty line of cupcakes or other baked goods that are special-order, seasonal, or customer-favorites -- the products that bring people back again and again. The key is to plan a menu not only around tastes, but profits. Another way to increase profits without increasing labor costs is to offer the right product mix of add-ons and special touches, such as deceptively simple decorations, ribbons, and rental fees.

While figuring out a break-even point is great for knowing the viability of a business, the reality is that for many people, starting a business is far more than breaking even! It is making a profit! A second approach to forecasting is to set the starting point at the amount of profit you want to make to meet your lifestyle goals and pay off any debt. This is "beginning with the end in mind." We all have our own ambitions and financial goals. Some people are just looking to supplement their family income and want the flexibility to work at home doing something they love. Others see the success of larger bakeries and want to be the next *Charm City Cakes*.

Questions to consider:

By answering the following questions you can help identify the necessary forecasting model for your business:

- How big do I want to grow?
- How much time do I want to put in on a daily basis?
- Do I have the necessary capital?

When you start at the end, you can better identify the necessary profit you want the business to generate during the calendar year. How much effort and capital will it take to produce that profit? How much sales revenue is necessary to support both profit and costs?

Projected Cash Flow

In simple terms, to pay your bills, you have to have more cash coming in than going out. Sometimes, when business is strong, supplies are plentiful, and labor is cheap, this is easy. More often than not however, it takes a watchful eye, fiscal restraint, and careful cash flow management to make sure the cash going out is not in excess of the cash flowing in. Businesses fail because they cannot pay their bills. Every part of your business plan is important, but none of it means a thing if you run out of cash.

The point of preparing a projected cash flow is to plan how much money you need before start-up, for preliminary expenses, operating expenses, and reserves. You should keep updating this information and using your projections after your business is up and running. A projected cash flow enables you to foresee shortages in time to do something about them--perhaps cut expenses, or negotiate a loan. But foremost, you shouldn't be taken by surprise.

There is no great trick to preparation: cash-flow projection is simply a forward look at your checking account. For each item, determine when you expect to receive cash (for sales), or when you will need to write a check (for expense items).

You should track essential operating data, which are not necessarily part of cash flow, but allow you to track items that have a heavy impact, such as daily sales and inventory purchases. You should also track cash outlays that will be necessary prior to opening in a pre-start-up column. This information should be in your start-up expenses plan.

Your cash flow will reveal whether your working capital is adequate. Clearly, if your projected cash balance ever goes negative, you will need more start-up capital. This plan will also predict when and how much you will need to borrow.

Explain your major assumptions and address any of the following questions:

- If you provide a restaurant cakes on wholesale order (on credit) in one month, when do you actually collect the cash?
- When you buy ingredients, do you pay in advance, upon delivery, or much later? How will this affect cash flow? Are some expenses payable in advance? When?
- Are there irregular expenses, such as quarterly tax payments, maintenance and repairs, or seasonal expenses, such as additional staff during the holidays, which should be budgeted?

Loan payments, equipment purchases, and owner's draws usually do not show on profit and loss statements, but they do remove cash and are therefore important to a cash flow projection. And of course, depreciation does not appear in the cash flow because you never write a check for it.

Table 5

		Month x	
		Budget	***Actual***
Revenue			
	Receipts		
	Cash Sales		
	Loans Received		
	Grants Received		
	Other Income		
	Capital Injected		

Asset Disposal		
Total Receipts	**$0.00**	**$0.00**
Payments		
Material Purchases - Cash		
Material Purchases - Creditors		
Sub-Contractors		
Audit / Accounting Fees		
Bus. Dev. - Travel		
Bus. Dev. - Entertainment		
Bus. Dev. - Meals		
Capital Acquisitions		
Charitable Contributions		
Commissions		
Conferences & Seminars		
Consulting Fees		
Depreciation	n/a	n/a
Employee Benefits		
Entertainment		
Equipment Lease		
Facilities - Insurance		
Facilities - Phone		
Facilities - Property Taxes		
Facilities - Rent		
Facilities - Security		
Facilities - Utilities		
Facility - Other		
Financial Charges		
Furniture		
Insurance		
IT Consulting		
Legal Fees		
Loan Capital		
Loan Interest		
Miscellaneous		
Office Supplies		
Payroll - Operational Staff		
Payroll - Administrative Staff		
Payroll - Owner /Directors		

Payroll - Sales /Marketing		
Payroll Taxes		
Postal / Shipping		
PR / Advertising		
Repairs & Maintenance		
Research & Development		
Storage		
Subscriptions & Dues		
Taxes & Licenses		
Telecommunications		
Vehicle Expenses		
Total Payments	$0.00	$0.00
Net Cash Flow	$0.00	$0.00
Opening Cash Balance	$0.00	$0.00
Receipts	$0.00	$0.00
Payments	$0.00	$0.00
Closing Cash Balance	$0.00	$0.00

Table 5: Projected Cash Flow

Opening Day Balance Sheet

A balance sheet is a fundamental financial report that all businesses need to understand and monitor the value of the business. If, for example, you are seeking a loan, the bank will use a balance sheet to assess your net worth and evaluate your credit-worthiness. In the most basic terms, a balance sheet is a list of everything of value -- your checking and savings account, mutual funds, house, cars, 401k-- that you own and a list of everything you owe to creditors -- mortgage, car payments, and other loans. You subtract everything you owe by all the stuff you have and arrive at your net worth. Remember, if you are seeking financing from a bank, they are looking at your personal finances. If this is a start-up business, there are probably no company assets or liabilities. If you are purchasing an existing cake business, then a balance sheet would be provided by the sellers, showing you what items of value are held by the company (assets), and its debts (liabilities). Just as with a personal balance sheet, when liabilities are subtracted from assets, the remainder is the owners' equity.

Use the spreadsheets provided in our website resources section as a guide to calculate your opening day balance sheet. When adding to your business plan, detail how you calculated the account balances. Optional: Some people want to add a projected balance sheet showing the estimated financial position of the business at the end of the first year. This is especially useful when selling your proposal to investors.

Table 6

Balance Sheet
[Mmmm Dd, 200X]

	Assets			
Current Assets:				
Cash			$0.00	
Accounts Receivable		$0.00		
Less:	Reserve for Bad Debts	$0.00	$0.00	
Merchandise Inventory			$0.00	
Prepaid Expenses			$0.00	
Notes Receivable			$0.00	
	Total Current Assets			$0.00
Fixed Assets:				
Vehicles		$0.00		
Less:	Accumulated Depreciation	$0.00	$0.00	
Furniture and Fixtures		$0.00		
Less:	Accumulated Depreciation	$0.00	$0.00	
Equipment		$0.00		
Less:	Accumulated Depreciation	$0.00	$0.00	
Buildings		$0.00		
Less:	Accumulated Depreciation	$0.00	$0.00	
Land			$0.00	
	Total Fixed Assets			$0.00
Other Assets:				

Goodwill	$0.00	
Total Other Assets		$0.00
Total Assets		$0.00
Liabilities and Capital		
Current Liabilities:		
Accounts Payable	$0.00	
Sales Taxes Payable	$0.00	
Payroll Taxes Payable	$0.00	
Accrued Wages Payable	$0.00	
Unearned Revenues	$0.00	
Short-Term Notes Payable	$0.00	
Short-Term Bank Loan Payable	$0.00	
Total Current Liabilities		$0.00
Long-Term Liabilities:		
Long-Term Notes Payable	$0.00	
Mortgage Payable	$0.00	
Total Long-Term Liabilities		$0.00
Total Liabilities		$0.00
Total Capital		$0.00
Capital:		
Equity	$0.00	
Net Profit	$0.00	
Total Capital		$0.00
Total Capital		$0.00

Table 6: Sample Balance Sheet

Business Plan Appendices

Often, there are documents that can inform your business plan and strategy, but don't seem to fit into one specific category. In this case, include these details and studies in an appendix. For example:

- Advertising materials
- Blueprints and plans of your shop
- Maps and photos of location
- Magazine or web articles
- Detailed lists of equipment owned or to be purchased
- Copies of leases and contracts
- Letters of support from future customers
- Any other materials needed to support the assumptions in this plan
- Market research studies
- List of assets available as collateral for a loan

5
FINANCING YOUR BUSINESS

We purposefully placed the chapter on writing your business plan before the chapter on funding your business, because you'll need to have a clear sense of the financials of your business–how much money you will need, how much money you have on hand, and your plans for earning revenue before you even consider funding your business. Once you have reviewed your costs as discussed in the previous chapter, you can determine the scale of business you will start and how much financing is required. For example, if you are starting a home business and determine all of your startup expenses to be about $7000 (Example 1) and your ongoing expenses to be about $300 a month, you will need about $9000 in total financing. This is because you should have at least six months worth of cash-on-hand to cover your expenses. ($7000 =[6 months x $300 = $1800]= $8800). It's risky to count on the sale of cakes this month to fund the next month's supplies and ingredients. Instead, you should have the cash in reserve. Tracking your cash flow is very important because you don't want to get stuck, low on cash, unable to purchase ingredients, supplies, etc.

As we explained in the chapter above, your business plan and forecasting will help you determine how many cakes, cupcakes, cake pops, etc., you will need to sell each month to cover your monthly expenses. Almost any business expert will advise you that it takes at least a year to start making a profit; therefore, you want to secure financing before you start your business in order to have the necessary cushion to see you through that first year (or more).

Funding Sources

When it comes to financing your cake business, there are a few options available to you:

- using your own credit cards and personal finances to open the business
- friends and family
- commercial financing from a bank or using an SBA-backed loan
- micro-lending and crowd-funding

• investors and angel investors

Each choice has its advantages and disadvantages.

Self-funding

Most small business owners end up using their own money to launch their business. This is because in many cases, commercial lenders balk at providing start-up capital for an unproven business that has no revenues to prove the loan will be repaid on time. For home-based cake businesses, the amount of start-up capital is far less than you will need if you are opening a commercial space; however, even the smallest businesses require some cash to get started. These costs include basics such as ingredients, as well as traditional business expenses, including an annual insurance policy, any licenses, permits or health department inspection fees, branding, advertising, packaging, and any expense related to getting your product to the consumer. For example, if you plan to sell online, you will need funds to cover the costs of a website; if you sell at local farmer's markets, there are likely annual or monthly dues; most cakes are delivered in boxes, etc. A complete list of expenses for a commercial bakery and a home operation is provided in **Chapter 13**, Expenses.

The biggest hurdle here is, of course, if you don't have your own money to use. If you don't have equity to pull out of your house or savings accounts from which to draw, you are like most people who want to start a business from the ground up. Don't be discouraged! People bootstrap new businesses every day. The key is using caution and preparing yourself with realistic data about your income and expenses.

The first advantage of using your personal finances to open your business is that you remain completely in control, creatively. You don't have to do anything to meet commercial lender requirements; you don't have to let an investment company control an interest in your business. If you can afford the investment, without affecting your quality of life, personally financing your venture (or personally financing it with the help of family or friends) might be the best option for you.

The second advantage of self-financing, at least in part, is that if you do want/need additional funding, it shows outside investors that you believe in your business enough to invest your own money. This is crudely known as "skin in the game," a term coined by Warren Buffet, meaning putting one's own money on the line just like outside investors. Even if you do have personal assets to leverage, you need to be careful. Businesses do fail, and if you've tied up your life savings in the business, you will lose more than a great idea.

The disadvantage to using personal finances to launch the business is that if you've tied up all of your assets, run up the balances on your credit cards, and pulled the equity out of your house, you'll have little left to make you credit-worthy when seeking commercial lending for a capital infusion or to grow the business. If, for some reason, it takes longer to start generating revenue than you expected, your personal credit could be tarnished in the process. That is why the amount of "skin in the game" is a balancing act -- putting enough of your own money to project the confidence you have in your cake business, but not so much that you've damaged your credit.

According to the SBA, 80% of all small businesses are funded all, or in part, with personal funds. If you plan to use your own money to start your cake business, it is wise to have access to cash upfront, and enough cash to last at least 6 months in business. You should not count on the sales of your cakes to fund your business immediately.

Exact dollar amounts for starting a cake business are difficult to project. A home-based business may be able to start with as little as $500 to invest in basic ingredients, licensing, permits and a farmers market fee, while a commercial operation could require tens of thousands of dollars, depending on the size of the business, its location, and the associated costs. If you don't have all the money you need, it may be possible to work something out with friends and family to assist with the rest.

Using Your 401(k) (or other retirement account)

In many cases, 401(k) savings can be used for small business start-up costs without being penalized for early withdraw or higher tax rates. Using your retirement to finance your business is a risk only you and your financial advisor can make, understanding that many businesses fail within the first year. However, many businesses fail because of a lack of capital; so, if you have a good business plan and just need the money to make it happen, it might be a worthwhile risk.

Since other lending options can come with as much risk as using 401(k) savings, it's often a very attractive choice. Not only do you avoid having to qualify for commercial lending or commit your personal assets to guarantee the loan, but you also avoid having to give up control to an investor.

There are two different ways you can use your 401(k) savings to start your business. In one method, the process is similar to taking a loan against your 401(k), but the maximum cash you can take is $50,000 or 50% of the balance of your 401(k), and if you default on the loan repayment, you'll be nailed with the extra taxes (unless you are over the age of 59½).

The other method may require the assistance of a CPA or tax attorney who is familiar with the ROBS loan (Rollovers as Business Start-Ups). In this method, a firm will help you create a 401(k) plan for your new business using the funds from your old 401(k). The 401(k) then purchases stock in the company, furnishing you with the start-up capital you need.

Friends and family

Interest rates are dismal for money sitting in savings accounts right now, making it an ideal opportunity for friends and family to take some of their savings and put it into your business for a better return. The advantage: you have a built-in level of trust. The disadvantage: if something goes wrong, you may live to regret it, especially when your uncle complains at every family reunion about how you took his money.

If you take a loan from a family member, the most important way you can protect your business and your relationship is to treat your family investor like a business partner.

Draw up a detailed contract that specifies how and when your lender will be repaid, how much interest will be paid, and what, if any, control the family member gains in your business. It's a good idea to have an attorney draw up your agreement. You don't want to over complicate such a contract, just get the specifics in writing. Don't think that because it's your parents or your cousin that money won't make it difficult to work out problems.

Woo Your Investors

When you are trying to attract friends and family to invest in your cake shop, you want to provide concrete reasons to invest, beyond your personal relationship. You need to present a solid business plan with revenue projections. You can enhance your appeal by providing references or letters from potential wholesale customers stating that they would purchase your cakes in bulk, or contract with you for catering services, parties, or weddings at the prices you have established.

Give Friends and Family a Role

Inviting a friend to work with your business in the capacity of an advisor can help elevate his or her interest in your success. Start-up companies can be an exciting challenge. It's where the dreams are. Your friends and family may be craving an opportunity to share hard-earned experience and knowledge with you, and once invested emotionally in your success, these individuals will often be more willing to invest financially as well.

Commercial Lenders

Retail cake shops are far more likely to require financing. Unfortunately, even for seasoned entrepreneurs, financing has been made more difficult in recent years. New due diligence requirements emerged out of the 2008-2009 economic recession, during which time credit and cash flow all but dried up.

It's not impossible to obtain financing to start your business, but to secure a loan, you need to be very clear about your business plan and be willing to commit your own resources to demonstrate your personal investment in the business.

It is a harsh reality for many aspiring business owners that commercial lenders are not in the start-up business investment industry. They lend money when they can guarantee to the best of their ability that the money will be repaid, with interest. Often, they will only loan to businesses that have been in business for at least three years. Remember, a commercial bank's goal is to achieve the highest possible rates of return, while mitigating risk.

If you are not an established business with provable revenue, you may find it difficult to obtain commercial lending. However, commercial lenders who participate with the Small Business Administration may be more willing to help with your business if you meet certain criteria. In most cases, though, if the business is not already up and running, you may have to guarantee the loan personally, meaning if the business goes under, you will be responsible for the loan payments.

Your business plan will be very important when applying for a loan. In addition to the documents from Chapter 3 that you've created, be sure to indicate in an appendix the amount of loan you are seeking, how the funds will be used, and the requested repayment terms (number of years to repay), collateral offered (home, automobile, etc.), and a list of all existing liens against collateral (e.g. existing loans).

For most businesses, the most common source of third-party financing is through the Small Business Administration (SBA). The SBA has two main programs available for business loans, the 7A and the 504. The SBA does not fund loans, but provides government guarantees to a portion of each loan made by private banks participating in the program.

To have the best possible shot at obtaining a commercial loan, having a solid business plan is absolutely essential. Your business plan should be well researched and contain an in-depth SWOT analysis. SWOT stands for strengths, weaknesses, opportunities, and threats. Strengths and weaknesses are internal factors. Opportunities and threats are external factors. The advantage of obtaining bank funding is the rapid funding of the loan and the ability to get up and running relatively quickly.

During the economic crisis of 2009, there was a 60% drop in SBA lending. Even when lending is not as restricted, typically owners must be "credit qualified" -- their personal credit rating must be high -- to qualify. The U.S. government has been crucial in the fight to secure additional credit opportunities for small businesses, encouraging the Small Business Administration to provide more government-backed loans.

There are two programs available from the SBA that often help small businesses with their financial needs, particularly if you are buying an existing bakery or cake shop with a history of profitability.

7A Loan Program

This loan program is the most flexible offering from the SBA and is designed to help existing small businesses obtain the financing they need, particularly if they are not eligible for other loans. Because the loans are designed to be flexible, they can be used in a variety of different industries for a number of purposes, including purchase. Loan terms are 10 years for capital and up to 25 years for assets.

Both commercial banks and non-bank lenders can participate in the 7A lending program, so the availability of the loans is increased. Even though the SBA guarantees a percentage of the loan, if a lender determines that the loan carries too much risk, the SBA cannot force them to give the loan. There are certain eligibility factors that must be met, but it is an excellent source of third-party financing in most cases.

504 Loan Program

The SBA 504 Loan program has much more specific criteria, including job creation requirements. The loans from this program are often targeted toward revitalization areas and are only available to for-profit businesses. As well, these loans must be used for fixed-asset projects.

Peer-to-Peer Lending

The advent of peer-to-peer lending has created new sources of funding for entrepreneurs. Sites like Prosper.com and Lending Club, work in the same way as an eBay auction. To get started, it is free to set up an account. Be sure to read each site's guidelines and the types of loans their lenders fund.

Prosper does not officially fund business loans, but they do fund entrepreneurs who want to start a small business. Once you have familiarized yourself with the system and browsed other successful listings, post the amount of the loan you need and the maximum interest rate you will pay on their online auction site. You want to convey with confidence and hard numbers, your proposal. You must have a good personal credit score to qualify for a loan, usually 640 or higher.

Your loan request will go into a 7-day auction. Lenders bid on your loan and, as they do, your interest rate may go down. If you change your mind and decide you don't want/need the loan, you can stop the auction.

The interest rate and monthly payments are fixed and there is a one-time closing fee. When paying back the loan, there is no charge for prepayment. The loan is unsecured, which means you do not have to put up any collateral to guarantee the loan. All of their loans are 3-year fully amortized loans funded through WebBank. To obtain a fair interest rate, however, you still need to have a strong personal credit rating. Rates can be as low as 7.5% for those with good credit, and can even be bid lower by lenders. The interest rate can be worse than credit card rates for those whose credit is rated a D or D-.

When you apply for a loan on Prosper, you provide profile information that authorizes Prosper to rate your credit based on an electronic credit check. There is no way to adjust the rating they give you, but you are allowed to explain your credit situation in your narrative.

Peer-to-peer lending organizations connect willing lenders and investors with borrowers who have the opportunity to make a more direct appeal to their potential investors.

Crowd-Funding

Kickstarter is a new approach to financing/fundraising dubbed "crowdfunding." It is basically an online threshold pledge system for funding creative projects including food-related projects and businesses. Projects funded on Kickstarter do not require repayment in the traditional sense, like peer-to-peer lending. In this model, a project creator develops a proposal (often relying on a video introduction and unique take on a business or creative endeavor). People who want to fund your business are offered unique products and experiences related to your progress.

Web Resource: Kickstarter.com

A few successful food-related projects include:

- Liz Chou's The Cake Chew - Changing the Way We Eat a Cake (kck.st/crHZlZ)
- Michael Pinckney's Taking Gourmet Cakes to the Streets! (kck.st/dLSmIr)
- Sabertooth Bakery! 100% vegan baked goods bicycle cart! (kck.st/h0zNkG)

Investors

Investors have a different perspective than commercial lenders. Investors typically provide funds needed in the short term, as they are looking for quick turn-around and they expect to share in the rewards.

In your business plan, indicate how your cake business would use any funds provided by investors; estimated return on investment; an exit strategy for investors (the method for recouping their investment); percent of ownership that you will give to investors; milestones or conditions that you will accept; financial reporting to be provided; involvement of investors on the board or in management.

Angel Investors

A commonly overlooked source of funding is that of angel investors. These investors, unlike commercial banks, are willing to take more extraordinary risk and will often provide funding for start-ups in exchange for some interest in the business. The advantage of this kind of funding is that no immediate payback, if any, is required. The disadvantage is, of course, someone else having any kind of say in the way you run your cake shop. However, these financial deals can often be structured in such a way as to meet everyone's approval.

When you do find an angel investor, you need to have some flexibility about the terms of the deal they will make with you. The advantage of an angel investor is that you get the cash you need without the pressure of repayment before you can make a profit. That advantage however, is often accompanied by the investor wanting some creative control or decision-making power. You need to decide what is important and what isn't before negotiating your deal.

Find Angels Online

Keep in mind that many angel investors want to make a difference. Do your homework and find angels who like to develop communities or help first-time entrepreneurs become business owners. The more you understand about how to appeal to your angel, the more likely it will be that you will be able to obtain some support in financing your dream.

Creative Approaches

Most small business start-ups have to use a variety of funding options to obtain the capital they need. One way to give people an incentive to invest is to sell "stock" in your company that provides a direct and ongoing benefit to the small community investor. This idea of selling community shares in your company is one way to raise money for your bakery's start-up costs. For example, a $500 investment could entitle the shareholder to one free cake a week, or a dozen cakes each year, plus a 10% discount for life.

6
CREATING YOUR CONCEPT

Figuring out what kind of cake business to open will be one of the most important decisions you'll make. It might seem obvious and you may already have strong ideas in your mind about your business, but writing them down is an important step. If you can't write about your concept, then it isn't clear enough. When something is crystal clear in your mind, you can express it succinctly and you will save time and money when you are ready to implement those ideas. Once you can express your concept, all other decisions will flow from it -- from the branding, to the kinds of cakes you will offer. The concept you choose should be something you love and something you are confident you can create. The branding elements you will use to communicate your concept will be addressed in the following chapter, but before you can create a brand, you need to think about the product.

Selecting a Menu

One of the first decisions you will make in your cake business is the selection of your cake recipes -- your menu. The decision-making process can be a fun way to draw friends and family members into your business and, in the process, gain a solid base of support. Those who are invited to help make recipe decisions in the beginning, will feel a sense of pride in your business and will be all the more likely to promote it and support it in the months and years ahead.

Determining what kind of menu you will have is both creative and strategic. Obviously, if you're famous for a certain cake recipe with your family and friends, it will probably be featured in your new business. However, menu planning is more than deciding upon products you want to sell. It is also about formulating and finalizing recipes, figuring food costs, and using your menu to inform the equipment selection. If you want to stay in business, you need to concentrate on planning a menu that allows you to earn enough profit to pay you, plus all of your monthly bills.

For example, you do not want to purchase expensive equipment that gets little use in your menu, or to spend too little on the equipment you will need extensively. Many first-time bakery owners save a few dollars on critical equipment such as mixers, ovens, and refrigeration, only to find out that repair costs or inefficiency actually costs them far more in lost revenue. Again, early menu planning will help you think through your recipes, the time to make batches, and the quantity you need to make (and sell) each day; therefore, your equipment must be able to support that quantity. Use the Cost of Goods process as discussed in Chapter 4 to help you determine the actual cost of each recipe. You know by now that the wedding cake industry is extremely competitive. Your menu is a huge part of determining your particular concept and will help you to differentiate yourself from other cake businesses.

Product Mix

There are so many possible recipes for a cake business that it can be difficult to know where to place your focus. As fun as the menu planning can be, determining your product mix is hard work that will require fine-tuning as you go. Part of what will determine your product mix is going back to the business plan and taking a close look at your target market and your competition. Remember, with your menu, you project a very specific kind of business. While your menu is critical to creating the concept, the most important thing to keep in mind is profitability.

It is important when planning your menu that you consider having some staple items that are less labor intensive and have a high profit margin. Your goal should be to balance your offering of profitable items with popular items. Consider the following when deciding on your product mix:

Difficulty of recipe – While there are some amazing cake recipes available, you need to ask yourself about the potential workload that more complex recipes require. As you read through recipes (including those on our website), consider the implications of the more labor intensive processes.

Refrigeration and freezing – Can the cake recipe you are considering withstand refrigeration/freezing when you have large/multiple orders, or you need to take a break.

Less is more – While you may dream of a rich variety of offerings, we recommend starting off with a few basic recipes.

Be known for something – What separates you from all the other cake businesses in town? When conducting your competitive analysis, look for an opening to fill an unmet market need.

Consistency – When you become known for a certain kind of product, it becomes much easier for a bride or a groom to recommend you. Your goal is to become the go to business for your niche. This doesn't mean you have to be the most expensive or the least expensive. Just be the best at what you offer.

Creating Room for Profit

Think about what you can make and sell that provides good margins. One way to help ensure that you keep the costs of production low and make it easier to make a profit on the items you sell is buying in bulk and using commercial size recipes. The recipes bakeries use most frequently cannot be duplicated using any commercial mix or combination of mix and "from scratch." If you are uncomfortable using mixes in your business, find recipes that are almost as quick and simple to prepare as a mix. In the costing exercise (Chapter 4) we broke down the cost of a delicious Champagne Cake. Depending on the volume of business you're doing and the scale of your pans, you may need to upscale your recipes to increase efficiency. Consult Professional Baking by Wayne Gisslen, for a detailed explanation of how to do this correctly. You can also find commercial recipes similar to your own kitchen recipes and do a little experimentation to perfect them. Recipe adjuster programs can help you make larger batches; however, you should always start with doubling and then test before tripling a recipe.

Web Resource: Commercial Recipe Calculator

There are many tools online for helping you turn home recipes into commercial-sized batches. One such recipe adjuster tool can be found at http://tinyurl.com/cakecon.

Finally, another way to help make profits easier is to streamline your production process. Most major restaurants understand the idea of streamlining; it is why they have prep cooks. The prep cooks are paid less than the chef, do most of the time-consuming work, and make it easy for meals to be prepared quickly during the peak times. The same concept can be applied to your cake business.

As you gain experience in cake decorating, you will develop your own strategies to work faster and more efficiently, thereby increasing your profit. The following tips are offered to assist you in reaching a level of time management in your cake decorating business that others obtain only through trial and error lots of time.

Mixing

- Have all tools, equipment, and pre-measured ingredients needed, on the counter.
- You don't want to waste time running around for ingredients, so make sure you have everything on hand.
- Keep ingredients at room temperature for best results. Eggs should only be left out about 30 minutes before using them.
- Scoop shortening from can to the measuring cup with a rubber scraper or spatula. Press it into the cup and level it off with the same spatula.
- Spray baking pans with non-stick product.
- When measuring flour, heap desired amount into measuring cup and scrape off the excess—do not pound or settle it.
- Sift flour, baking soda, baking powder, and spices to avoid lumps
- Mix chopped nuts, dried fruit, or other additions with a little of the flour used in the recipe to keep them from sinking to the bottom as they bake.
- Test your baking powder or soda to see if it still has leavening power by adding a small amount to a bit of very hot water. If it bubbles and fizzes, then it's still good.
- Err on the side of under-mixing - don't over-mix.
- Double check to make sure you did not leave out an ingredient.

Baking

- Before mixing batter, preheat the oven, prepare cake pans, and move oven rack to center position.
- Try a No-Stick Spray and follow with a light dusting of flour for greasing cake pans.
- Place cake pans at least 1 inch apart from each other and from the oven walls. This allows air to circulate.

Frosting

- Crumb coat: to seal in crumbs, spread a thin layer of frosting on the cake, and then refrigerate it. When the base coat of frosting is hard, spread on a final, heavier layer.
- A seemingly simple decorating skill that can become very frustrating to a new cake decorator is the process of coating a cake smoothly. Thanks to the internet there are many useful tutorials demonstrating this process. Practice makes perfect.
    - http://tinyurl.com/cakebusiness7

- http://tinyurl.com/cakesmooth

Don't Procrastinate

As soon as an order is taken, begin a list of the steps you can do ahead of time. The goal is to keep your actual decorating time to a minimum during the final days and hours before delivery or pick-up.

Royal Icing

When planning a cake design, always consider which elements of design can be created ahead of time. Since royal icing hardens when dry, decorations can be made in advance of the cake and stored for weeks in an airtight container. Flowers, ribbon, bows, lettering, and color-flow work can be prepared weeks in advance, allowed to dry, and simply placed on the iced cake before delivery.

Gumpaste

Gumpaste decorations can also be made weeks in advance and temporarily stored in airtight containers, or kept there indefinitely away from heat or moisture. Always offer gumpaste as an option to your clients, as items such as flowers can look very realistic. Gumpaste is a profitable medium in which to work and classes can help you streamline your efforts for increased profitability.

Boxes and Boards

Once the cake design is planned and all possible decorations have been made in advance, still more work can be completed before the final days. If you have plenty of room, assemble the cake box and affix at least three of your business cards to the top.
The cake board can also be prepared in advance. If plywood needs to be cut to size, go to the hardware store and have it cut. When you are using cardboard or foam core board, cut the board yourself with a craft knife. Cover the board with fabric, wrapping paper, or other material. Complete the board with a covering of cellophane and ribbon glued around the edges.

Refrigerating and Freezing

Several days before baking and decorating, mix buttercream icing and refrigerate. The day before decorating, divide icing into smaller bowls and color with paste food coloring. Store tightly covered in fridge. Bring to room temperature on decorating day.

Whenever possible, avoid baking ahead of time and freezing. However, just about everybody freezes their cakes when their business picks up! When volume of business increases and wedding cake orders start coming in, freezing can become unavoidable in many cases. The cake must be protected from freezer condensation by using a moisture-proof wrapping. Suggested wrappings include:

- greaseproof paper thoroughly covering the cake and taped

- aluminum foil, or aluminum foil and plastic wrap/greaseproof paper underneath it
- plastic self-sealing bag

When freezing cake layers, cool completely and wrap tightly in plastic wrap. Do not freeze iced cakes. When thawing, remove from freezer and set on a flat surface (kitchen counter or tabletop). Do not remove any of the wrapping until completely thawed. Be careful. You don't want to lose the cakes you now urgently need!

Questions to consider:

•If you are still in the early stages of your bakery and haven't nailed down your concept, review the following questions to aid your thought process:

- What kind of customer are you trying to attract?
- What kind of businesses are you trying to emulate?
- Will you cater events and/or take special orders for weddings and other parties, or will you have a few select designs and flavors?
- If you are a home-based operation, will you require a minimum order? Will you deliver? Can customers order online? Will you sell at farmer's markets?
- When people order cakes from you, how will it be packaged; will you have rental items such as cake stands plateaus and plates?

Pricing

Pricing is one of those difficult topics like sex, religion, and politics. People are reluctant to discuss it openly, but very opinionated. It is as much an art form, as it is a science and no one algorithm can guarantee an optimal price. That said, we recommend avoiding the common advice given on web forums of adding up all of your ingredients then doubling, tripling, etc. for a profit. Calculating your prices can be anxiety provoking, making you feel that you are doing it wrong, but don't avoid the difficult task of doing the math and testing various estimates. We've provided a few examples below. What you're aiming for at this point is an estimate. More importantly, what you want to avoid is underpricing your cakes and losing money. Try a couple of these strategies to see if you can't reach the price that not only guarantees you a profit, but also seems reasonable in your market.

The easiest method is using your competitive analysis to set your prices close to those of your competitors. Make sure that your analysis really compares the same quality and type of product you plan to sell. This method should only be used as a starting point because there are too many unknowns when comparing what you will make with a competitor.

The more accurate method and the one we recommend is starting with the costing method demonstrated in Chapter 4. A costing calculator or formula will help you determine what price you need to sell your product to break even. Remember, breaking even is the baseline. Many novices fail to calculate in a way that at least enables them to reach this baseline. Costing a recipe ensures you are covering the raw material costs of producing a single serving of one of your cakes (cupcakes, cake pops, etc.).

The next step is to add in the cost of the other variable expenses in making your product. This includes the costs of running (or renting) your kitchen, utilities, as well as your hourly wage. Some cake pricing calculators will include these variables. We think it is critical to account for your own labor costs when pricing a cake. Be sure to include both the time baking and decorating the cake, as well as the client interactions, delivery, billing, and follow-up. Often, the time spent on a cake out of the kitchen can increase the price significantly. For example, an order that comes in over the phone with very simple instructions and is picked-up in a few days is far less time consuming than a wedding cake that requires an initial consultation, delivery, and follow-up.

In the beginning, adding 100% of your labor costs may be unrealistic, as it will likely take you longer to produce your cakes and thus, will price you out of the market. As you gain more experience the speed with which you can bake and decorate your products will increase. Nevertheless, you should keep track of the time and the hourly wage to get a realistic sense of how much money you are making per hour.

Next, you should account for your overhead or fixed costs. These include your start up costs and ongoing expenses. Obviously, overhead costs for a home business will be far less then if you were operating in a commercial kitchen.

At this point you should have two figures:

- Variable expenses (the expenses for an individual cake)
- Fixed expenses. (the expenses that do not change, no matter how many cakes you make).

There are several ways to use these figures in determining your pricing. The first way is probably the simplest.

1. Divide your fixed expenses for the year by the number of cakes you would produce in that same time. For example, if you have $1000 in annual overhead expenses and you make 50 cakes per year, your per cake expense is $20. For each cake you make, add on $20 to account for overhead. Pretty simple right?

2. The second approach uses an algorithm that is a bit more complex, though it accomplishes the same objective more accurately. You will need to spend some time accumulating costs collected from real numbers. In this approach, you add up all of the variable costs for the entire year. Then, divide your total fixed costs by the variable costs for the year. The result is the amount that you would add to each dollar in variable cost when calculating the price.

Fixed costs	$1000
Variable costs	$14850

([$75 (ingredients) + ($200 labor) + ($10 utilities) + ($2 paper goods) + ($10 fuel) average]) x 50 cakes per year = $14850. Keep in mind this is greatly simplifying the match, as it is unlikely you would make 50 identical cakes. You want to track down the numbers that closely approximate the kind of business you plan to do.

Divide total annual fixed costs by the total variable costs:

Divide total annual fixed costs by the total variable costs:

$1000 ÷ $14850 = $.07

For every dollar spent on producing a cake you must add seven cents of fixed cost for that cake.

If we use the example from above, we would add $20.79 (in fixed costs)

Here's the math:

($75+$200+$10+$2+$10= $297)

Total variable cost per cake: $297

For every dollar, add $.07 or $297 x .07= $20.79

$297 + 20.79 =

Total cost of cake: 319.79

OK. Now you have acquired the baseline, or break-even price for this cake. Any price below this is a loss and any price above is profit. The question at this point is what should you charge in order to make a reasonable profit? Again, the simplest approach would be to take the industry standards of 5-10% net profit margin. However, if you have conducted your competitive analysis thoroughly, you should have a clear understanding of the clientele you expect to serve, the value of the products you make and what the market will really bear. Keep in mind that gourmet cakes and cupcakes are part of nearly every wedding celebration. A cake is both a luxury and a necessity. Check out prices for specialty cakes on the internet in communities similar to yours. As part of your competitive analysis, you will research various grocery stores, bakeries, and other at-home bakers to get an idea of their prices for cakes and cupcakes. You should plan on researching as many cake companies as possible. If you are comfortable calling these businesses all over the country, ask the employees or owners to give you an idea of what at-home bakeries charge.

When you have a good representation of several bakers' prices, begin calculating your costs to determine your own prices. In the United States, as elsewhere, prices for such specialty items will vary from town to town, city to city, state to state. Thoroughly research the prices in your area to determine a price that will be both within reason to most buyers, and profitable to you. You may find that your market can bear more than the industry standard, 5-10% profit, particularly if you are a home-based business.

Other Menu Planning Considerations

You will never be able to please everyone who walks through your door or visits your website, so don't even try. You'll quickly go out of business trying to keep enough supplies on hand to meet the tastes of everyone. Instead, have a clear vision of what type of cake business you are and then perfect it.

Comparing Apples and Oranges

As you compare your figures with the list of prices that you obtained by calling various bakeries, remember--they are not your "competition":

- You offer one-of-a-kind cakes available nowhere else.
- You offer a better-tasting product.
- You offer the best and freshest ingredients.
- You offer personalized customer service.
- You offer delivery and display set-up.
- You offer a one-on-one relationship with the customer.
- "Money Is No Object!"

Your cakes must taste so delicious, that once a customer has been introduced to your products, nothing else will suffice. Customers will come to you time after time because they love your cakes and nothing else will do!

Cake Business Niches

There are some obvious cake niches:

- Wedding cakes
- Occasion cakes
- Birthday cakes
- Cupcakes
- Cake Pops

Specialized niches.

Many startups are approaching the cake business by looking at specialized areas, such as specific diets. Focusing in on one area may help you have a unique perspective on the industry, potentially inventing new ideas for products. Consider that the cake pop only recently became a huge phenomenon when Bakerella introduced it on her blog a few years ago.

Health-Oreinted

Of course the traditional cake is typically high in sugar, fat, and calories and meant to represent an indulgence at a celebration. More and more people however, expect food producers (even cake decorators) to offer health-conscious options. This might include allergy specific offerings such as gluten free or diet, and lifestyle cake options such as vegan. An organic cake might contain spelt instead of refined white flour, and carob instead of chocolate. To help control portion size, many celebrations provide small cupcakes instead of large servings of cake. Do not forget foods that are whole grain, chemical free, locally sourced, vegan, and organic.

Allergies, special diets and health related concerns

As a parent of a child with Type 1 Diabetes, I understand the impact of a single piece of cake in a child's diet. Undoubtedly, you will deal with customers who have specific issues and requirements around the food they consume or serve to their guests. Unfortunately, as a service provider you are unable to accommodate every client and every situation. That said, the more information you can provide, the more value you are creating for your community. Take for example the common peanut allergy in small children. By providing clear labeling on your products you can help consumers avoid a dangerous exposure to nuts. Likewise, providing nutritional information on your cakes and cupcakes will help carb counting families. These are small, but meaningful efforts that will help your customers and distinguish you from your competition.

Seasonal

Many home-based bakers create a dedicated following of return customers by emphasizing cakes that correspond to the seasons. For example, fruitcakes and buche de noel during the winter holidays, Valentines cakes in February, Easter bunny cakes in the spring, Mothers day, fresh fruit inspired cakes in the summer, and anything apple or pumpkin in the fall!

Sculptural

Some cake businesses emphasize the trend towards creating edible 3D sculptures from cake, popularized by Charm City Cake founder Duff Goldman on Ace of Cakes. These cakes are custom designed and labor intensive, but given their popularity, could be a viable niche for you.

Keep a notebook of cake ideas to supplement your growing library of recipe books, periodicals, and website references. The notebook might contain color copies of photographs of your own products, clippings of articles from baking and business magazines, printouts from the web, and an index of product ideas, recipes, innovative cakes, etc.

Maintaining an index of product ideas allows you to quickly reference photos and articles that inspire you. Divide this notebook into headings or categories for quick reference. Your index headings will develop as you find product ideas that you like and may consider adding to your product line in the future. Examples of headings might include:

- Organic
- Gourmet
- Icings
- Fillings
- Chocolate
- Nuts
- Bar cakes
- Seasonal
- Gift Packages
- Wholesale Ideas
- Packaging Ideas

A system of 3-ring binders works best, since you can carry them anywhere, make copies, insert loose sheets, and refer to your records at a moment's notice. You can learn more about this in Chapter 16.

Cake Ingredients

When choosing a recipe, keep in mind some practical matters. Consider the list of ingredients: are all of the ingredients readily available from your supplier? Are the ingredients reasonably priced? Is your recipe traditional enough to be enjoyed by a wide audience, yet sophisticated enough to be unique? Consider the method and time required to prepare the dough. Does the recipe require starting with a cold oven? When your business takes off, you will be mixing and putting new pans of cake batter into your already-hot oven, one after the other. You cannot afford to wait for the oven to cool down.

Does the recipe require folding, stirring, or other time-consuming, hand mixing methods? Many excellent cakes are prepared using a simple dump-and-mix method: dump all the ingredients in the bowl and mix. Choose the latter to maintain a speedy work flow.

When the cake comes out of the oven, consider texture and taste. Will yours be thin and crispy, thick and chewy, or somewhere in between? Will your cakes stand up to shipping?

Taste can vary, depending on the flavorings used. A basic sugar cake recipe can be prepared using vanilla, lemon, or almond flavoring. When you find a recipe that tastes great with vanilla flavoring, experiment with other flavorings to be sure they all taste great.

Keep it Simple

When choosing recipes, you may be tempted to start with extravagant and decadent recipes. Although you may want to set yourself apart by offering the most luxurious cakes in your area, be advised that most people prefer one of three or maybe four options: sugar cakes, chocolate chip, shortbread and brownies. Build your business around a few simple recipes, as they will account for a huge percentage of your orders.

The three basic recipes in your arsenal should include very simple ingredients and be quick and easy to prepare. Again, stick to the basics. On rare occasions you may need other recipes, but at least 95% of your cakes will use these three or four recipes.

The reason you will use the same recipes again and again is because your clients will generally come to you after they have seen and tasted your cakes somewhere else (not your shop or home) and they will want exactly what they enjoyed at the party, wedding, restaurant, or store. Given their delight with the cake they have just tasted, it is the same recipe they will choose for their own needs--whether for a small birthday or a dinner for 250 guests. If you are always changing recipes, you will inevitably disappoint some customers and may be viewed as unreliable. On the other hand, you should keep your selection fresh and interesting-- both to you and your customers. You will soon learn which recipes are the "classics."

Develop a Product Guide

When you're ready to start marketing your products to businesses and retail customers, you'll want to provide them with a product list/price list. The first step in your marketing strategy is naming your products.

Name Your Products

Select imaginative and personalized names for your products. Be sure to include some descriptors that enable the customer to make an informed choice. Get creative and come up with fun names that will make your cakes stand out from the store-bought brands. Consumers these days know that a unique name often equates to a special recipe and quality ingredients.

A product and price list is both practical and necessary to pique the interest of your potential clients. This list is simply a reference when discussing product options and taking orders from customers. Some orders are received via telephone, so it is helpful if the customer has a list to choose from. A great way to promote and advertise your product and price list is via the internet. Customers can see the product, the ingredients, a picture, and the price list. Many orders will also be taken in person as you go around to businesses in search of long-term customers. Your product and price list should include:

Name of Cake – This is the creative name you've given to your products. Ideally, you should include a picture.

Ingredients – Include the ingredients and highlight the special ingredients that may be unique to your product, such as organic or locally produced items. For example, for a Maple Cream cake, highlight the origin of the maple syrup produced in a quaint New England community.

Options for Ordering – If you have special options such as a minimum order, or if you are willing to make substitutions in your products, you should let the customer know.

Price – You should make a price list by the item and by the dozen. Make a separate price list for wholesale and retail customers. Remember, only wholesale clients should ever have access to the wholesale price list.

Labels for Your Cakes – What is on your labels can be just as important as the quality of your product inside. It is an entire marketing segment that you should study. Make sure all of your contact information is easily visible to promote repeat business.

Ideally, include the following information on each and every label or tag:

- Company name
- Logo

- Name of cake and any applicable expiration date
- Ingredients
- Phone number
- Email
- Website address

As more communities enact cottage bakery laws, the labeling requirements are becoming more standardized. You should check with your state health or agriculture office to confirm the format of your labels. A label can be attached to the cake box. Many states require the following:

- The name and address of the your operation
- The common name of the product (e.g. chocolate cake)
- The ingredients of your cake, in descending order of predominance by weight
- The net weight or net volume of the cakes in the package
- Allergen information as specified by federal labeling requirements

If any nutritional claim is made (low-fat), appropriate nutritional information as specified by federal labeling requirements

The following statement printed in at least 10-point type in a color that provides a clear contrast to the background label: "**Made in a cottage food operation that is not subject to state food safety regulations.**"

Federal Allergen Labeling Information – All cottage food products must be labeled in accordance with the United States Code of Federal Regulations Title 21, Part 101. As a cottage food operator, you must identify if any of your ingredients are made from one of the following food groups: eggs, milk, wheat, peanuts, soybeans, fish, and tree nuts. In a sample label provided on our website, possible allergens are identified as "Contains wheat, eggs, milk, soy, and walnuts." This labeling allows consumers to avoid food which may be harmful to them.

7
DEVELOPING YOUR BRAND

Your brand should emerge from your concept as its public facing expression. If your concept has a 'traditional', homemade vibe, then you may want your business name, logo, products, etc., to reflect that aesthetic. Being home-based does not necessarily mean old-fashioned or stodgy. If your emphasis is something contemporary and hip, you can imagine how the look and feel would be different. This chapter addresses branding elements and collateral of your cake business.

Naming Your Business

Deciding on a business name is often one of the first things people think about when starting their business. It is not a simple decision to make, because your business name will establish potential clients' first impressions of you. Taking the time to investigate the successful and unsuccessful names of other companies is an often-neglected step. In today's age of internet searches and social media it is also important to select a business name that can be translated to a web address and Facebook page.

Even if you're not ready to launch on the Internet, reserving the name you wish to use is a prudent step. You don't want someone else registering your domain, so it is wise to buy your domain name as soon as possible. Check with the domain name registrar godaddy.com to see if the name you like, or some derivation of it, is available. If your domain name is already taken, there are creative ways such as adding geographic terms or a dash in order to secure an available URL. For example, if PaulasCakes.com is taken, an alternate might be PaulasCakesVT.com, or paulas-cakes.com.

You want customers to remember you, so be creative. Because of the nature of a cake business, you can really play with words to generate something unique. While you would never want to copy a name that already exists, research the names of cake businesses online. There are delightful examples that may help you brainstorm. Be sure to ask the advice of family and friends for their thoughts on your business name. Brainstorming always works better in groups and with people you can trust.

Again, with a creative name, you will establish name recognition for your business more quickly. When naming your business, you may also want to avoid selecting a personal name, like Rachael's Homemade Cakes. While you may have a lovely name, it may get lost in the sea of other businesses. (This is not a steadfast rule, particularly if you can integrate it into a creative theme where your identity is part of the brand -- think Paula Dean, Famous Amos or Martha Stewart.) Try to be really innovative. Avoid names too closely related to existing businesses. While a name may be available to use in your state, you can still have legal trouble if the name infringes upon the trademark of another business. Simply stated, you can't use a name (or logo, slogan, appearance, signage, or product name) that can be easily confused with a competing bakery that has registered that trademark.

Even if they have not registered a trademark, an existing business is protected by unfair competition laws. For example, if you select the name Awesome Cakes and there is a bakery in your community called Awesome Bakery, you would likely be subject to a trademark infringement or an unfair competition suit. Even though the names are unique and the word Awesome is common, the fact that both businesses sell baked goods could cause customer confusion. Selecting a name that is not only available in your state, has an available URL, and has a very low likelihood of causing any customer confusion takes time to research, but will avoid legal trouble down the road.

Also keep in mind the impact of your business name in your customers' minds. Is it memorable, whimsical, and easy to spell? Does it capture the essence of the cakes you sell? Will your business name stand the test of time if you grow into other product areas? It might be tough to sell wedding cakes if your name is Awesome Cake Pops.

Business Name Registration

If you choose to present yourself under any name other than your proper legal name, you will have to register your fictitious business name. This is typically handled at the county level, or if you are registering a corporation, at the state level. First, conduct a search through the county or state database (usually online) to make sure the name is not already in use. Then, there is a simple form to fill out and a fee (anywhere from $10 to $100). Some states may have other requirements, such as publishing the notification in a local newspaper classifieds. Your county clerk's office will provide the details about the process in your area. The Appendix also lists each state's registration office for LLCs and corporations.

Developing Your Image

Logo

One of the most critical graphic design elements of your branding strategy is your logo. Your logo is your identity in the same way as your business name. In fact, if your design is successful, people are just as likely to associate you with your logo as they are with your name. Consider how many food companies are recognized around the globe by their signature logos.

For example, Coca-Cola's red and white script and unique bottle, McDonald's golden arches, Quaker Oats' smiling Quaker, are all symbols that have grown in our consciousness and have enabled their associated brands to grow in consumer loyalty and profit. If you take the time to think about the significance of logos, no matter what the brand, you can understand how they are created to inspire trust, recognition and even admiration.

Your logo should be unique enough to make people think of your business every time they see it, but not so confusing or complicated that your customers won't know what it is.

For a specialty cake shop, something that is associated with the type of product you sell or induces your customers to think of your name is important. For example, if you are primarily a business focusing on traditional homemade celebration cakes, incorporate that into your look. If you plan to emphasize weddings, these cakes can evoke a kind of elegance or sophistication. If you plan to offer a high energy, playful kind of experience in your shop, you might incorporate colorful, whimsical elements in the design.

A logo is so important that you may want to outsource this effort to a professional designer. The internet has made it much easier and more cost-effective to find suitable designers who can help you create this kind of branding collateral.

If you are familiar with local design resources, it is nice to be able to meet with someone in person; however, if you've never hired a graphic artist, the internet enables you to draw from a huge pool of talent; and thus, more people are competing for your graphic design business. The result is higher quality work, more choices, and lower costs.

Web Resources: Logo Designers

99 Designs [http://99designs.com/]

Logo Factory [http://www.thelogofactory.com/]

Logo Bee [http://www.logobee.com]

Logo Loft [http://www.logoloft.com]

Even if you are hiring someone to do design work, you should educate yourself about what constitutes an effective logo, and remain active in the process. Do not hesitate to ask questions, provide criticism, and get the results you want. If there is something your designer provides that you do not understand or with which you disagree, make them explain their thinking. This is a give-and-take relationship, and one for which you are paying. Additionally, when you have some comps to look at, don't make the decision alone. Sharing the design options (before a decision is made) with friends, family, or people whose taste you trust is invaluable. When someone offers you their opinion, they will often point out things that you did not even see or consider about the design.

Here are a few simple guidelines to follow when choosing (or designing) your logo:

- A logo must be able to be described accurately in a single sentence or phrase. If your logo can't be translated into words with ease, it won't be effective as a marketing tool. Your customers should be able to understand and share the concept of your logo: "A big pink box," "A happy child eating a cake pop with a smile on his face."
- A logo must be memorable. This is subjective, but if your first impression says, "this is too generic," then ask for alternatives. Keep in mind, memorable does not necessarily mean complex. In fact, a simple logo can be easier to reproduce and, more importantly, easier to remember. Examples: Apple, Nike.
- A logo must be effective without color. You are potentially going to be putting your logo on cards, boxes, cups, napkins, aprons, on doors and windows – everywhere. Your logo (or a version of it) should be just as effective coming from a stamp as it is from a four-color press.
- A logo must be scalable. Again, because your logo will be used many places, it needs to be just as recognizable when it is an inch high, as when it is 20 feet high.

When evaluating designs keep in mind that the logo:

- Looks good on print materials (business cards, letterhead, invoices), as well as on your website
- Could be made into a sign
- Should be delivered in vector format as well as layered psd (Photoshop document) and .jpg
- Is easy to distinguish from your competitors

Your logo will be used in all of your marketing materials, so it needs to portray the essence (concept) of your business. Keep language and text separate from your logo. A textual treatment of your company name, e.g. "Sweet Bites" is a common part of many logos. It's best to keep the visual and text elements separate (as opposed to overlapping, intertwining, etc). This way, you'll be able to use either the text or icon independently.

Likewise, your "tagline" -- the phrase or few words that describe your cakes -- should also be distinct elements. Your tagline or business name can be featured with your logo; but, if they are required elements, then at smaller sizes they will require a small font that will become illegible.

Text can also create a lot of visual clutter in many applications. There are appropriate places to use your tag line, like your website and business cards. Once you have created a logo, it should be placed on all materials: labels, order forms, signs, tags, business cards, brochures, stickers, etc. Your logo is critical to product recognition. Some people respond to words, while many others respond to images. Even if a customer can't remember the name, they'll remember the logo.

Cost-saving idea: Create a black and white logo that can be printed in a variety of colors, made into a rubber stamp, printed on a black and white printer, etc. Sometimes, the simplest tools are the best. If, for example, you provide cake boxes for customers on the go, don't spend money on printing stickers in the early days of your business. Use your simple stamp logo on invoices, flyers, letterhead or even business cards. Reserve the full logo for your door, website, press kit and sign.

Signage

If you will open a retail location, purchasing signage for your new business is a must. It can be expensive, but it is not a cost you should put off for too long. Think about the businesses that you visit, both at home and when traveling. Isn't signage one of the most obvious ways we distinguish one place from another?

Being visible in your community is one of the most critical factors for the success of a retail cake business. For any kind of bakery, a good location combined with visible, well-designed signage can help drive traffic to your business, eliminating some of the need for costly marketing campaigns.

Before you invest in any signage, check the code regulations of your area. What type of sign has your city council, county planners, or historic preservation commissioners deemed acceptable? Usually, your landlord can provide you with the necessary guidelines and local zoning ordinances which regulate the type, size, the height, the configuration, the color, the aesthetics, etc., of signage.

For example, if you have neon in mind, and the local historic commission only permits low profile placards, you want to know that before investing in something that will end up in your garage, rather than the front of your cake business. Once you know the rules, you can approach a vendor. Chances are, if the vendor is local, they are familiar with the Uniform

Building Code [UBC] and local zoning requirements of your area. As long as you purchase or lease your sign from a reputable company, you should have no problems. Make sure that your contract with the sign company includes a clause that they are responsible for your sign meeting local requirements. Moreover, make sure the clause makes the company liable should any adjustment in your sign be necessary due to zoning regulations or other city or county codes. The company should also obtain the necessary construction and installation permits.

A well-conceived sign can be an excellent marketing tool. It should not only be reflective of the image you wish to project, but communicate important information about your business. Again, is there a vibe to your shop that you want to project -- upscale, hip, gourmet, etc.? Put it on the sign. Signs communicate important information to potential customers. The sign should say something to draw in the customers in your immediate area. Signage should be an important part of the promotional strategy in your business plan and should be included in your loan package.

There are other ways in which a sign compliments your business: it reinforces the other outreach tools, such as your logo. Consumers who find you online, for example, will have greater ease finding your cake business if the logo is used on your sign. In fact, your logo design and your sign should be similar, if not exact. You are creating a brand and an integrated marketing plan. Your customers will remember your logo, colors, and fonts, so choose them carefully.

A sign that is clearly visible from the road gives motorists ample time to stop and park, so be sure to use a typeface that is legible from a distance. Cursive or intricate fonts can be hard to read in any presentation. A sign is a visual cue that customers can remember, encouraging repeat business. A visible sign that is easy to understand can make the difference between success and failure. Many businesses attribute a large percentage of their business to their signs. Once you have invested in a sign, it is to your advantage to keep it in good repair. If you lease through a reputable sign company, the maintenance of the sign can be made part of the contract. A dilapidated sign does not send the right message for a successful business. So, factor maintenance into your costs if you will buy instead of lease. In addition to your location, signage can make the difference between success and failure.

Even if you are a home business, you may need a sign if you plan to sell at farmer's markets or other venues. The best option in this case is a vinyl printed banner, available from online printing companies. Our favorite is GotPrint.net. We use them to print all of our postcards and business cards. GotPrint offers fast turnaround and great products. Be sure to request a sample pack so you can see and feel all the papers and items in person before you buy.

8
MARKETING

Without a doubt, there is a huge market for beautifully decorated, custom-made cakes, cupcakes, and more. The key is reaching the people who want to buy from you. As a cake business owner, your job is not only about making great products; you are also a marketing strategist. This means simply, you have to get the word out there about your new business. In the early stages, most businesses require a great deal of marketing. This chapter covers all of the different facets of marketing, including social media, traditional advertising, community outreach, and brand awareness.

Social Media Marketing

By now, you should be well aware of the impact the internet can have on launching your small business. Your customers use the web more than any other medium to research the products and services they are considering. This is true both for major brands and local mom-and-pop bakeries. Social media has leveled the playing field for small businesses to reach big audiences. You can use this medium to build momentum for your business before it even opens. Start to let people know of your plans, menu ideas, stories about yourself, and the steps you're taking each week. The goal with social media is to build a community of fans or followers who will grow with you, buy from you, and refer your products to their friends.

Twitter

The free social networking site, Twitter is a favorite among foodies and new food entrepreneurs. You can easily get started by going to Twitter.com and opening an account. Use your business name when selecting a username and be sure to fill out the profile describing your business. If you are already a Twitter user, use this section as a gut check on how effectively you're using it. If you are new to Twitter, the concept is to create a network of people with similar interests, who follow you. For a boutique cake business, this network might include people interested in cake decorating and baking in general, your shop and products, small business, marketing, baking, industry trends, and lastly, your local community. You want to get local users to keep you in mind for their next occasion, so connect with them first on Twitter.

The easiest way to start (once you've created an account) is by searching subjects of interest at search.twitter.com. Read the posts of others and follow people of interest. Again, you should follow people in your community as well as people and businesses worldwide. In turn, they can choose to follow you. Often other users will automatically follow you, but sometimes they like to read the kind of posts you make, so don't hesitate to start making observations, joining conversations, and contributing. By posting and following, you build a network much in the same way you build business and customer connections in the real world. The more value you add in creating informative posts, the more people will follow you. It seems difficult at first when no one is following you, but surprisingly, people will find you and want to follow you.

Be sure to educate yourself more thoroughly about Twitter functionality such as Sponsored Tweets, ReTweeting, Hashtags, Direct Messages, Twitter Lists, Location Services, and more.

Twitter Simplified

How do you transform followers into customers? When you post about your business or community, or offer specials and news about your business, it keeps your treats in the minds of potential customers. Thus, the larger your following is, the greater your chances are for bringing in business that day. This is not an excuse to spam. It is a process that builds slowly and must be nurtured.

Especially when you have a physical location, you want to advertise how your patrons can follow you on Facebook and Twitter. This can be as simple as mentioning your Facebook and Twitter names at your store, or in the window of your shop. Likewise, on your website, you want to encourage prospective customers to follow you. Give them a reason. Post a daily coupon code on Twitter and give a free treat to the first five people in the door who mention the code. Countless bakeries post updates on Twitter when products are fresh out the oven, or when new flavors are offered.

If people are interested in what you write about, they will follow you. An added element of Twitter is direct messaging. Often your followers will send you direct messages. This could be simply to say hello, or potentially to request something from you. A small bakery in Charlotte, NC doubled their clientele by finding and following local Twitter users, and then inviting them to place orders via Twitter. Customers can place an order from their phone or computer and the bakery has the order waiting when they walk through the door.

Why is Twitter so valuable? Research suggests that only 14% of people trust advertisements, while 78% of people trust the advice or recommendations of other real consumers. Your brief tweets are distributed both directly to people who have asked to receive information from you and, more importantly, those messages can be passed on with a click of a button to many new potential customers.

Use Twitter to educate customers about your cake business. Engage in the conversations they're having about your neighborhood and establish yourself as someone who cares about the community. Listen to what your customers want. Social media is a great opportunity to discover new innovations. It enables you to hear what people are saying about your business. If it is negative, get in there and address the situation. Speak one-to-one with your customers, and show your concern for what they think. In the same light, don't hesitate to thank other users for their praise.

In the early stages of planning your business, Twitter can be a great opportunity to ask people in your community what they want from a local cake business. Do some sample "testing" of ideas. Figure out what is important – price, novel recipes, locally sourced ingredients, maybe even great coffee for folks stopping into the shop or picking up an order from your home operation? Develop relationships with others in the business. And most importantly, give people something to talk about and a reason to buy from you.

Facebook

Developing a Facebook page for your business is an important step that is technically simple, but requires some finesse to be effective. Facebook pages are often a business' second home on the web. Unless you are well versed in social media marketing, it is important to keep a few guidelines in mind when using Facebook (or any social network) in your marketing plan. First of all, an online social network is surprisingly similar to offline networking. Just because you are behind a keyboard, rather than face-to-face, does not mean that you should disregard established conventions. Many businesses want to make an impact quickly and mistake social networking as an opportunity to start advertising to a large audience.

Social marketing requires an investment in time. Your network on Facebook, many of whom may be customers, are looking for value from any social networking relationship. They are experienced enough to know if someone in their network simply wants to spam them with advertising, rather than creating real value. For it to be worthwhile for anyone other than friends and family to join your network, you need to have two-way conversations and provide value. If you are unfamiliar with social networking and marketing, here are some simple ways to use Facebook effectively:

Put all of your contact information on your page. While your fan/business page is a great start, customers want to learn more about you. Make it easy for them to get to know you and your business. Include your URL so people can find your website. Write in a simple, direct way. Your business description should be written not only for those who already know you, but also potential customers. If you are open for business, make it obvious where you are located, your hours of operation (if you have a store front), and what kind of cakes or other products and services you offer.

Post same-day news about special products, flavors, discounts, coupons, etc. Once you've made the effort to attract a fan base, you need to keep them engaged with frequent posts; otherwise, they will lose interest in your business. Are you trying a new recipe? Do you have a limited supply of a special product? What inspires you? Tell your fans.

Post photographs. Nothing grabs our attention and whets our appetite like stunning images of people's personal creations. Remember, Facebook is a means of getting people in your shop or in the mood for your one-of-a-kind cakes. Seeing your confections is an effective way to draw an audience to your physical location.

Write about a variety of topics -- not just your products. Mix product-related posts with topics that share your personality. For example, you can write about behind-the-scenes details such as how you got started, new business developments in your neighborhood, special ingredients you're trying, etc. People love to hear about the "romantic" aspects of operating a business. Your posts on Facebook can sell not just individual products, but your shop as a destination. What do you love about owning a business? Make your post something readers/ fans look forward to seeing.

Ask your customers for advice. Today's consumers love to be invited into the process. Look for opportunities when your customers can provide feedback. For example, you could seek advice about new flavors. In an environment with such creativity and such a range of tastes, a cake business can reinforce the loyalty of your clients by making them feel invested.

Become connected with fans of other local businesses, other cake companies, bakeries, or home businesses. Remember, using Facebook effectively means viewing it not just for marketing, but also as a community-building tool. Interact with other businesses by referring clients to them, or by asking and answering questions. Facebook is a wonderful opportunity to provide support to your fellow bakers and local businesses. See what they're doing online and offline, offer ideas and form a community.

Your business page and your personal page should be kept separate. Configure the privacy settings on your personal page to allow visibility only to friends. You might support certain political or social causes on your personal page, but your business page should be all about your products and services and include a link to your website.

While some may argue that social media is not critical to success, there are too many examples of small businesses like bakeries, cake companies, healthy food companies, and other types of business, that have launched entirely on the internet and then grown into brick-and-mortar operations. Moreover, there are examples of bakeries across the world that have harnessed social media so successfully that it is a primary marketing channel on par with -- and sometimes exceeding --all other traditional media. There are even stories of bakeries that were on the verge of failure, only to reach out to their online networks to be saved by a viral outpouring of support. For these reasons, social media marketing should be the foundation of your marketing effort.

Online Marketing

Neither home-based nor brick-and-mortar businesses can survive well without broadening their reach through online marketing and the development of a clean, easy-to-navigate, well-organized website.

Website

Your website is all about branding your business, making you recognizable, and telling your story. The two most common ways to establish a web presence are building a site from scratch using HTML, or using a content management system that enables you to plug your information into pre-defined content areas. The first method requires that you have the skills to build a site or that you hire someone, while the second method incorporates the free publishing platform, Wordpress. We recommend the latter, as Wordpress is easy to use, installed quickly, highly customizable, and search-engine friendly.

The first step, as suggested before, is to buy a domain. Your domain name (which can cost as little as $10 per year) is ideally the same as your business name. Unfortunately, many of the best domain names are taken. Sometimes, investors purchase common names with the hope of selling them to authentic businesses with the same name, and for significant profit. Occasionally, names are purchased, and then later abandoned. You can research names that will soon be available on pool.com and namejet.com.

Your presence on the web is your public face. It tells prospective customers who you are, where you're located, what you sell, and how much your goods might cost. Most importantly, it enables the customer to see pictures of your cakes, an important selling point. Wordpress sites are great for branding and offer elegant, business-oriented themes to give your site a unique look. Think of your website as part advertisement and part information. Your goal should be:

- Explain what kinds of products and services you offer, and convey a message of why the customer will benefit from choosing you.
- Create a website that is easy to navigate, with tabs or links to additional pages that are clearly marked. Include relevant contact information.
- Connect to your blog, social media, and other relevant information on the web establishing you as a professional and sharing a bit of your personality.

Your website does not work just as a marketing tool with your customers. It also establishes your credibility within your industry, with your vendors, and for networking purposes. A website is flexible enough that it can be used in a number of ways. You may wish to work with the media, go to trade shows, contact buyers directly, and use it to impress financial backers.

Online Directories

A free source of online advertising is a business listing in the local directories of Google, Yahoo, Bing, etc. Once you've invested the time and expense in creating a great website for your business, you want to make sure it gets traffic. These directories are a great way to increase your exposure, and often allow customers to add comments and ratings, which you can encourage your satisfied customers to do, in order to help grow your reputation.

Getting your business listed on the local search engines sites will not only get more traffic to your website, but -- more importantly -- more calls on the phone and more new customers in the door. Local search listings include your basic contact information, as well as a map of your business location. These listings are often given a very prominent position in the search engine results and they are free!

Web Resource: Local Directories

Google: http://www.google.com/local/add/businessCenter

Yahoo:http://listings.local.yahoo.com/overview.php

YP.com: https://adsolutions.yp.com/listings/basic

Bing: http://www.bing.com/businessportal/

Blog

Adding a blog to your website is another great way to communicate with customers and establish yourself as a reliable expert. You don't have to wait until you're in business to start reaching out to your community. Blogging is used by many successful business owners to attract an audience before they've even opened. Once you are established, blogging will increase the number of visitors to your website. Many small businesses struggle with the lack of search engine visibility for their website. They spend time and money in developing an internet presence, yet Google and Yahoo do not rank their sites very high using the search terms that will bring potential new customers. According to a 2011 HubSpot survey, companies that blog have far better marketing results. Specifically, the average company that blogs has:

- 55% more visitors
- 97% more inbound links
- 434% more indexed pages

What this means is blogging will increase the likelihood that when people in your community look online for cakes, your business comes up on the first page in the search. The major search engines are looking for relevant content. When you take the time to write about your latest creations, special ingredients you're incorporating, beautiful photographs of your cakes, or simply future developments with your cake business, the search engine "spiders" are identifying your site as an authority on a particular subject. The main thing is that there is activity on your site and that the text is related to the search terms your prospective customers seek.

If you feel like website optimization is too difficult, you can work with a writer or an SEO expert. The objective is to develop a set of keywords or phrases that describe your business and can be incorporated into your blog articles to help drive the right kind of traffic to your website. The most obvious keywords you should target are "cakes" + your community. (e.g. 'cake decorators in Atlanta' or 'wedding cakes Syracuse'). Additionally, the area in which you specialize, be it healthy cakes, gluten-free cakes, or some other differentiated niche, should also be emphasized in the topics of your blog.

Think about how the customer searches for a product and write down those words (keywords). Incorporate these keywords into your website text.

Offline/Local Marketing

Long before social media and the web, there were many effective ways of reaching a target market that are still important marketing activities. Local, offline efforts are essential.

Business Cards

The simplest step in marketing your business locally should be to carry and hand out business cards on a regular basis. Carry inexpensive business cards with you everywhere and give those cards to everyone with whom you come in contact. Speak with everyone you encounter during your day. Ask them what they do. When you have listened with sincere interest, they will usually ask what you do. Share your excitement about your new cake business! Curious people are often fascinated by the profession of cake decorating and want to hear more. People also like to do business with someone they have met. Be yourself and your sincerity will come through. Hand this person your business card and invite them to check out your website or give you a call.

Letter of Introduction

The next effort is to let all of your friends and acquaintances know about your new business by writing a letter.

Start by creating a list of everyone you know; you may be surprised by how many people you come up with! You will probably have no problem at all coming up with an initial list of at least one hundred names when you include:

- Your family members (in-laws and out-laws alike!)
- Neighbors -- include everyone on the address lists of your neighborhood association, your community pool, or club.
- Friends from church
- Friends from your former jobs
- Friends from your spouse's job
- Parents of your children's friends -- use address lists from school, soccer team, gymnastics, Girl Scouts, Boy Scouts, etc.
- Your roommate's family, friends, and co-workers
- Social clubs/sports clubs
- Your family's doctors, dentists, orthodontist, etc.
- Your attorney, insurance agent

We recommend sending a physical letter as the first announcement of your business, as it will stand out from the common electronic communication everyone receives daily. Although you will send the same letter to each person on your list, take the time to print each letter individually, including each recipient's name and complete mailing address, and printing his or her name at the greeting line (i.e., Dear Gail, not Dear Friends). Take the time to sign each letter individually. With your home computer and a good printer, you can produce a great-looking letter yourself, without the expense of ordering professionally printed letterhead. The following is a sample of an introductory letter that you may use or revise to better fit your business:

> Mrs. Jane Doe
> 1234 Main Street
> City, State 12345
>
> Dear Jane,
>
> I am excited to tell you about my new cake business, "[Your business name]."
>
> Made from scratch using the freshest ingredients, each cake is a unique work of art and can be decorated for any occasion: birthdays, baby showers, office parties, weddings, etc. It is often said about my delicious decorated cakes that they are "too pretty to eat," but please, enjoy! We also carry a complete line of cupcakes, cake-pops, and succulent triple chocolate brownies.
>
> When your next special occasion approaches, I hope you will call me. It would be my pleasure to provide homemade cakes for you and your guests.
>
> I have enclosed a few business cards. Please keep one for yourself and share the others with your friends and associates.
>
> Thank you for your support of my new business.
>
> Have a delicious day!
>
> *Jane Smith*
>
> Enclosures
>
> P.S. As an additional service, delivery is available to your home or office.

Sample Introductory Letter

When you have a final draft that reads exactly as you want, proofread it several times. When you are sure the letter is just right, print a personalized copy of the letter to everyone on your list. Be very careful to type in the addresses and names perfectly. Make sure your envelopes look just as professional and error-free as each letter. The letter (and envelope) represents you and your business. Time and money spent to ensure that your letter is totally professional and perfect leaves no doubt in your potential customer's mind about your meticulous attention to detail. Keep careful records of all expenses involved in this mailing for tax purposes: the cost of paper and envelopes, postage, etc.

After you mail this initial batch of letters, continue to add to your list the names and addresses of new friends you meet each day. When a family member brings home a new address list from a new club or team, add those names to your list and send each of them a letter as well.

Follow-Up Phone Call or Email

As is true with sales in many businesses, prospective customers usually need several contacts before finally placing an order. After sending the introductory letter, follow up with a telephone call or email within a couple of weeks. The purpose of this communication is to make sure they received your letter and to ask if they have a need for cakes in the near future. These follow-ups will probably not produce a lot of orders -- they are simply one more contact to remind potential customers of your availability.

The Power of Postcards

You've sent the intro letter and have called or emailed the potential customer. Your next step is to send a postcard or email about once every three months. The purpose of these communications is to remind people of your cake business continually, so that when they have a cake occasion, they will call you. Free services such as MailChimp, make sending mass emails easy and unobtrusive.

You can create your own postcards by purchasing 8-1/2" x 11" card stock and printing four cards on each page. As with the letter, make sure it's error-free. Your postcards should be different every time you do a mailing. Keep each card simple and quick to read. An example might be:

Your Business Name

Beautiful and Delicious Cakes

For All Occasions

555.777.1234

Delivery Available to Your Home, Office,
School or Organization

Ordering special cakes for a special occasion is often left until the last minute. You may include on your postcard mailings a phrase such as "Advance orders are appreciated. Last-minute orders are OK, too!"

Every piece of mail, email, phone call, and business card that you hand out is one more reminder to a potential customer that you are available for their next cake occasion. Make it your mission to keep your business name and telephone number in front of everyone you meet.

Press Kits to Food Editors: Create a list of every newspaper, local blog (e.g. patch.com), and television station within "cake pick-up or delivery distance" of your home. Take that stack of newspapers you accumulated when researching your ad strategy and look up the editor of the food or lifestyle section. They may be interested in featuring a story about easy cake decorating tips or perhaps an article on a home-based business.

Don't be intimidated by the words "press kit." You can create an online press kit by converting a Word or Google Document into a PDF and linking to it on your website. A physical press kit is simply the same document printed out and placed into a pocket folder. In your press kit include the following:

- A page that concisely describes your business (include your mission statement).
- A biography about yourself. Include a few paragraphs about how you started the business (your transition from the office or stay-at-home mom to at-home business owner., etc.)
- At least one excellent photograph of a close-up display of your finest cakes.
- A well-written letter of introduction.

Each sheet of paper and photograph should include your business name, your name, your e-mail address, and your daytime telephone number. Place a perfectly printed label on the front of the folder with your contact information.

Each sheet of paper and photograph should include your business name, your name, your e-mail address, and your daytime telephone number. Place a perfectly printed label on the front of the folder with your contact information.

After sending (or linking to) the press kit to an editor, follow up seven to ten days later with a telephone call to confirm their receipt of your press kit. Ask the editor if he or she sees the possibility of a story about a cake business or small business owners in the future. Keep your conversation brief and to the point. Whether the editor is encouraging or not, be very professional. Thank editors for their time and say that you would appreciate them keeping your information on file. You may hear from an editor a week later or a year later. If you do not hear back right away, you may send a short letter every six months just to keep yourself in the forefront of their mind.

Local early morning and mid-day news programs, local cable TV shows, and other locally produced television shows often produce segments focusing on general interest topics such as health, safety, food, fun projects for kids, home businesses, etc. The producers of these shows must create new and interesting segments for every single show, five days a week. Why not offer to do a segment demonstrating easy cake decorating techniques that viewers can try at home, a segment on home businesses, or stay-at-home parents who have started their own home businesses?

Call television or cable stations and ask for the name and address of these shows' producers or segment producers. Send your press kit with a cover letter to the appropriate person. Follow up two weeks later with a telephone call. Before placing this call, jot down your ideas on the type of segment you could do on this producer's show. Be prepared to share your ideas in one or two sentences. Segment ideas might include completing the decorations on three or four cakes for children's birthday parties, or demonstrating unique cake decorations.

If you reach the producer's voice mail, be prepared to leave a brief, concise message, but do not "pitch" your specific segment ideas. Speak confidently, clearly, and with a friendly tone. Be sure to mention your name, company name, telephone number, and the reason for your call: "I'm calling to follow-up on the press kit that I mailed you two weeks ago. I would like to talk to you about the possibility of a segment on cake business or home businesses when you have a moment to return my call."

Press Releases

Publishing press releases about your business is another way to take advantage of both online and offline marketing. Press releases can be submitted to your local newspaper, announcing the opening of your business, specials you are offering, or events in which your business is involved. You can include coupons or special offers in your locally printed press releases as well.

Some entrepreneurs fail to take advantage of the potential of a press release, assuming they are not relevant in the age of the internet. However, local newspapers still rely on press releases and many online resources pull information from press release aggregators or hubs as a way to research new content. While email marketing, social networking, Twitter, and other web-based opportunities should be incorporated into your overall marketing approach, traditional media such as newspaper and television should not be overlooked. Thus, a well-written press release is an integral part of your overall press kit.

Online, your press release can be submitted to both free and paid submission services and include links to your website, which improves your page's search engine ranking. Prweb.com is one of the best-known press release distribution services.

Web Resource: Press Release Aggregator

Prlog.org

While there are many paid services, Prlog is one of the top free resources for submitting press releases.

Your goal is to be the first item on the list when someone is looking for cakes in your area. You can publish press releases regularly, focusing on an event, holiday, or happening in your business. Most online press release submission sites also allow photos, which give you the opportunity to show off your cakes.

Advertising

If your budget permits, you can reach your audience via paid advertising. Through advertisements in the print media, brochures and online (e.g. Google Adwords) you can highlight your cakes to a wide range of people.

When you are ready to start investing in advertising, a great way to begin is by talking with similar businesses to find out where they advertise. Also, search the keywords your customers are likely to use on Google. Do other local cake or bakery businesses show up in the Sponsored Results?

Web Resource: Google Keyword Tool

http://bit.ly/MULJgT

The Google Keyword Tool gives fantastic insights into the search history of the keywords for which you want to rank well and the estimated cost per click for each.

Ads in Local Newspapers and blogs: If you can get a copy of the newspaper, look up the cost of ads. If you don't have a copy of the paper, call or e-mail the newspaper offices to determine their ad rates. Blogs often publish their ad rates. A simple ad can be inexpensive and sometimes free. When placing an ad, order it to run as long as possible. A one-time ad is not nearly as effective as an ad that readers see over and over again.

Newsletters: When you receive newsletters or learn about a newsletter, find out if they allow ads. Newsletters may reach a smaller group of people, but larger ads in a newsletter can be very inexpensive. Know the target audience of the newsletter before making a decision. If one newsletter goes to members of your local Bar Association, and another goes to mothers of twin club members, you may want to give more serious consideration to the moms who plan birthday parties!

Refrigerator Magnets: Turn your business card into a refrigerator magnet by affixing a business card-sized magnet to the back of your card. These magnets can be purchased at office supply stores pre-cut to fit your card, or you can purchase magnets in large sheets and cut them down. Just another reminder where your customer is most likely to see it! The magnets can be given to each customer when they pick up their cakes (along with other "plain" business cards to give to the guests at their party). They can also be included in letters to potential clients.

Local Outreach

To entrench yourself in your community and be the business that comes to mind first when people look for great cakes, there are things you can do each day to foster good relations in your community. These marketing benefits can't be beat.

Sponsorships: Sponsoring a local community sports club or putting an ad in your local high school's play program each year can add tremendous visibility for very little cost, while fostering good will. There are so many different opportunities in this area; you will want to choose one or two that mean something to you and be willing and able to say no. Try to identify low-cost-high-visibility sponsorship opportunities at first.

Chamber of Commerce Membership: For the small membership fee, you get the benefit of not only having a voice in the business decisions that affect your community, but you have unlimited networking possibilities with the business people in your town. Being a member of the Chamber of Commerce also gives you access to business resources and supports.

Yelp and Angie's List: You can create free business listings on Yelp and Angie's List enabling customers to review your products and services. There is no better validation of your cakes' quality than the social proof of an unbiased review. Make sure you follow up on all reviews. If you ever receive negative feedback, don't take it personally. Address it and correct the condition that made the negative review possible. Reach out to the individual, if possible, and publicly resolve the problem.

Better Business Bureau: In any service industry, but perhaps even more so with a business in the food and wedding industries, membership in the Better Business Bureau can be an invaluable source of developing customer loyalty. Simply by knowing that you are willing to comply by their standards can make your customers more comfortable with you. You must be in business at least a year to qualify and annual dues are required.

Charity Events: While it may seem like marketing is all about spending money, it's really about visibility. You do not have to spend a lot of money to be involved in your community in the ways that really matter. Depending on the size of your town or neighborhood and the reach of your business, you can choose which charities fit with your business.

Becoming involved in your local Relay for Life or helping to raise funds for the March of Dimes or a local children's hospital, can help establish you as a business that cares about more than profits… and that goes a long way toward developing customer loyalty.

Customer Service: Customer service is also an important aspect of word of mouth marketing. Good customer service is one of those intangibles of running a food business that many people assume they understand because they have experience as a consumer. We know good customer service when we see it, and we know bad customer service when we experience it. Now that you are the one behind the counter, you should review your assumptions and more importantly, write down your process and policies for your employees to be as vigilant as you in creating positive customer experiences. Never more than now, in the age of internet reviews, Yelp.com, Twitter, and social networking, has a commitment to superior customer service been so important to a bakery's success.

Satisfaction Guarantee: What will you do when a mistake happens? Create a policy, in writing, to inform your customers of your excellent satisfaction guarantee. For example, explain your policy if you make an error. For extreme errors, offer the choice of a partial refund, complimentary items, or a credit for free cakes in the future. Of course, individual circumstances require individual solutions, but it is a good idea to let customers and potential customers know you respect the adage "the customer is always right", and that you will fix any problems that arise.

Reputation Management: The key to maintaining a good reputation is a quality product and great customer service. A positive demeanor, quick response to customer concerns, and friendly service in all situations are critical. The way to protect your business is to anticipate/brainstorm every possible customer situation, create a written manual, and train your employees in these processes. If you cater, make sure all of your policies are included in a contract or agreement signed by both parties. At all times be courteous, inquisitive, and respectful. If you've made an honest mistake, own up to it; offer the proper remuneration and move on.

Word gets around quickly when a business owner or employee behind the counter is less than pleasant. In the same vein, word also gets around when a cake business has not only great products, but also friendly service. When it is a real pleasure to do business with you, your customers will return more frequently and refer new people to you. Whether you're a one-man or one-woman shop, or have a team of employees, even more important than the quality of your product is the quality of your customer service. Customers should be greeted with smiles, welcomed like long-lost friends, and catered to as much as possible. The experience they have every time they walk through the door, call you on the phone, or visit your website, makes a difference about what kind of business you have the next year.

Creative Marketing Ideas

Whether your business is located in a tiny town or a large metropolitan area, you can use creative marketing ideas to let people know about your services. Small towns may offer an advantage in some ways; you can become a big fish in a small pond. Even if your town is home to a company that has been producing specialty food or gift products for years, if you are savvy, persistent, and consistent in your marketing plan, your business can grow and become well-established.

Office Parties: If you've ever worked in an office, you know that birthdays are often celebrated with cakes or baked goods for the office staff to share. Some offices bring in treats for everyone's birthday; others have a party once a month to recognize everyone who has a birthday that month. Instead of expending the company's time (time is money) by having an employee go to a bakery or grocery store, why not have delicious cakes delivered to the office -- by you?

Home Party Plan: A marketing plan that has worked for many companies is the "home party" plan. A home party plan for your cake business may include a cake decorating demonstration, a display of your product line, your scrapbook to showcase your skills and, of course, the cakes that you bring for refreshments. Guests can order cakes for an upcoming event, but the primary purpose of this party is to allow potential customers to see and, most importantly, taste your cakes.

The results of the party will be seen in the coming months when those guests who were first introduced to your cakes at the party begin planning their next celebration.

Teaching: Another way to create awareness about your business, as well as an additional source of income, is teaching. Classes can be held in your home, church fellowship hall, community social hall, or other such facility. Schedule a date for your first class, determine the maximum number of students you are willing to accept (a good number is between 4 and 8 students for your first class), outline your class syllabus, determine your costs and class tuition amount, and publicize far and wide.

Start jotting down a list of everyone you know, every client, everyone who has ever tasted your cakes. Create a simple 4.25" x 5.5" postcard using white card stock. List the class title and description, date, time, place, and supplies students should bring, cost (be sure to mention if this cost includes supplies), your name, and phone number. State that class size is limited and specify a date by which students must register. When students call to register, remind them that no one other than paid students may come to class (i.e., no friends or children). This technique is under-utilized by many bakers because they fear creating more competition. The reality is that no one can make cakes like you. Demonstrating your expertise leads to more people who want what only you can provide.

Speaking: If you are teaching, the next step is even easier -- speaking. As a speaker, you are not selling a product (cakes); you are selling your expertise about a topic that your audience enjoys. There are many groups that would be fascinated by the topic of cake decorating. Everyone loves a cake! You can demonstrate cake decorating techniques, share lots of "tricks of the trade," and top it off with a cake tasting. Garden clubs, country clubs, and church groups often have speakers at their meetings -- and your topic is unique and delightful! You might also consider cake-making demonstrations and mini-classes at children's birthday parties and child care centers. The speaker fee and future orders from the guests at your workshop will surely add to your business income.

You may live in a large city where storefront bakeries or other home businesses abound. Do not allow yourself to be intimidated by the competition. Develop a marketing strategy and work on it every week. Furthermore, you can learn from others, networking and sharing information with similar businesses. As you are getting started, let them know of your business so there is nothing to hide. I wouldn't recommend asking a competitor to share hard-won details about their business, but there is plenty you can glean from paying attention each time you have an interaction.

As you explore various marketing opportunities, you may begin to see a pattern of one or two of your ideas producing more results than others. Pay close attention to which marketing strategies work best for you and focus on those strategies. Pay attention to the demographics of the majority of your customers. Do your services appeal to a specific socio-economic group? If you increase your advertising to that population, you may discover a niche market for your business that will provide a large portion of your orders. Cater to that niche while continuing to market to other groups.

9
SALES

Wedding Cakes

Wedding cakes can be the most lucrative of all your products if marketed and priced properly. In order to close the deal for many of your customers, you will need to conduct a cake consultation. Sometimes the bride, or someone making decisions about the wedding, has visited your website and will request more information (prices) via email or phone. If your designs and price range seem to fit the bill, your potential clients will want to meet with you in person to discuss their cake. Even in our internet-driven economy, wedding cake consultations are a huge part of making a sale. Consultations are sometimes conducted totally by phone and sometimes face-to-face in your home or shop. When setting the appointment for a consultation, ask the bride to bring any photographs or magazine clippings, sketches, etc—whatever is needed to communicate what her wedding is in her mind. Sometimes, she will have provided a link to a cake she's found online.

In the meeting, you will be reviewing all the details, decorations, and colors. Ask her to bring any fabric swatches (or even paint chips) if she wants color in her cake design. If she already bought a cake topper or other ornaments for her cake, she should bring them as well.

Cake Tastings

Tastings are not required, but in most places they are still the convention in some form or another. Tastings are a tradition. Prospective brides and grooms are getting excited about their impending nuptials and many like to be catered to. This is a great opportunity to impart an intangible sense of trust – that is, the client can determine if they can trust you with this part of their celebration. The customer service you provide here will often be the difference between you and the bakery up the street. Some bakers provide a cupcake or two of their most popular cakes. Others provide a slice of what they have on hand.

Basics of the cake consultation

- A cake tasting is usually the first step toward making sure the finished cake is exactly what the client wants. The bride and or groom will sample one to three different cake flavors that you offer, and you will work together to figure out the costs for their cake. When serving cake, it's also nice to serve hot coffee or tea and water.
- One way you can set yourself apart from other bakeries is to discuss openly and honestly the clients' budget. If you are genuinely concerned about accommodating their budget, your sincerity will come through. Being up-front with your clients regarding pricing is the best way to avoid misunderstandings later.
- Some clients will want to view photographs of your recent work to weigh in on quality and workmanship of the finished products and ask for references from past couples who've hired you.

You will want to display some of your designs on dummy cakes. Others can be seen in photographs. The dummy cakes simply show a selection of your most popular designs and the quality of your techniques. If a custom cake is to be served, I suggest a 6" round two-layer cake, simply decorated. You may choose to charge a modest fee to cover costs. Serve the cake and beverages as soon as everyone is seated. Since this is not a social visit, waste no time asking for their thoughts on the cake they are tasting.

Be Prepared:

There are also certain questions that you should be prepared to answer regarding the baking procedures:

- Are cakes baked fresh or baked in advance and frozen?
- Are the cake layers and icings made from scratch? If so, what are the ingredients? (This may be an uncomfortable question if you use a mix, but I think it is a fair question that you should answer honestly.)
- How many cakes do you design per weekend?
- Do you have a current Department of Health or Agriculture certification?

Be prepared for compliments, as well as criticism. Everyone has an opinion and if you have difficulty hearing someone expressing a critique of your cake, then tastings under these conditions may not be a good idea for you. (A common one is: "The icing is too sweet," or "I prefer [your competition]'s buttercream.") Keep in mind that this is not personal. Do not be discouraged. You have an opportunity to educate them so I recommend simply moving forward with the decision-making part of consultation. At this point, there are several key areas that should be discussed:

Design style: Have her bring photos/magazine clippings of design elements she likes

Size/servings: This is usually based on estimated number of guests

Types of frostings: Buttercream, fondant, royal icing

Cake flavors and fillings

Accents: Fresh flowers, gumpaste flowers, edible beading

Cake topper styles: Traditional, fresh floral, sugared fruit

This is the beginning point of recording their specific ideas for their cake on the contract. Start the process by asking your client basic questions. The most obvious being:

- How many guests are you expecting at the reception? (This will tell you about the possible designs of the cake, number of tiers, etc.)
- Do you prefer round or square cakes, fondant or buttercream?
- Which flavor did you prefer?

The key is to keep the process moving forward by only ever asking them to choose between a couple things at a time, while referring to the dummy cakes and samples they've tasted. When choosing flavors, you want to start with the bottom tier because typically it is the largest and what most of the guests will be eating. It seems obvious, but ask your client to consider which flavor her guests will enjoy the most. Then, discuss the filling, followed by the design and accents of the cake.

Begin filling in the blanks on the agreement and discuss the cost of everything as you go along. Remember to be especially tactful and sensitive when discussing your cancellation policy. Make sure you mention it, but don't dwell on it.

A very important part of your agreement is the list of telephone numbers of various people that you may need to contact before the wedding and possibly on the day of the wedding. If all of those names and numbers are not yet known, be sure to follow up later. The discussion of the cake size and artistic design of the cake can be very quick and easy if a couple comes with pictures and firm ideas. However, this can become a long, drawn-out discussion if you are not prepared to step in as the professional and help the client reach a decision.

You should not open your design idea books unless it becomes necessary. Ask the bride if she has seen a cake she likes or if she wants to start from scratch. Do not have all of your design idea books on the table, just your photo book of the cakes you've made. Once you have an inkling of the cake design likes and dislikes of the bride, narrow the search and the discussion. Offering too many choices can paralyze the client's decision-making ability. When design discussions begin, refer to the decorated dummy cakes. Obviously, the dummies and the cakes in the portfolio will be easy and comfortable for you to do because you've done them before. If you need to look further, go to your portfolio.

If the bride finds a design that she loves, encourage her to finalize her decision because continuing to pour through a library of photo books can become very time-consuming and even confusing. Another approach is to have her place a post-it note over the images she prefers, then cluster and narrow the choices from there. Once the design decision is made, be very careful to put every minute detail on the agreement, using separate pages if necessary. Include your sketches, magazine clippings, photographs, and any other relevant material. It is very important to note the size and shape of each tier requested, as well as all design details. Write them down.

If the couple desires a groom's cake, the same attention to detail is necessary as you complete the section of the agreement for this second cake.

At this point, some calculations will be necessary. Ideally, you can quote a price without hesitation. However, if you have been asked to do something unusual or exotic, don't feel rushed to provide a quote. You may need to do some pricing research. You can always contact the bride with the exact quote the next day. You should continue to fill out the agreement completely, even without the price. That way, if she is agreeable to the price, you can get a deposit and send it over to her immediately. Scanning and sending via email is the easiest way to send the proposal.

If she has selected a cake for which you are confident about the price, then agreement should be completely filled in. Ask the bride if she would like to go ahead and reserve her wedding date on your calendar today by signing the agreement and paying a deposit. As your business grows, you will be able to mention, "Dates are filling up fast." This isn't a "hard sell" per se, just the truth. When the agreement has been signed, make a copy for the bride. If you do not have a copier (or fax or printer that makes copies), assure the bride that you will mail her a copy of the contract within a few days. Often contracts can be completed in Microsoft Word and can therefore be emailed.

Occasionally, a bride will have already set up a consultation with another cake decorator and will prefer to wait before signing the agreement. This is all part of being in a service business – particularly the wedding service business. Brides will want to check out at least one other shop before making a firm decision. (Don't take it personally. It's not about you or your cakes.) It often depends on how prepared the bride is. If they are organized and have plenty of time to shop for services, they'll shop around. If time is of the essence, they may be ready to sign the contract and leave a deposit.

Whether or not the bride leaves you with a signed agreement and check (or credit card deposit), remind her that you are available if she has any questions and, again, offer your best wishes. If the agreement has been signed, send the bride a letter thanking her for the honor of creating her wedding cake(s) and list any details that she needs to provide for you-such as a final decision on her cake board design or her cake topper. If she does not yet have a copy of the agreement, mail a copy as an enclosure with this letter.

If the bride left the consultation without having made her final decision, send an email immediately thanking her for her time in coming to discuss her wedding cake. If she left with any unanswered questions, provide the information she needed. Remind her that you are available by telephone and e-mail to answer any questions she may have and wish her well as she plans her special day. Make it your mission to become "known" as the cake decorator whose cakes are both gorgeous and delicious and that you are a provider of EXCELLENT customer service.

Going Wholesale

Another place to sell your cakes is to restaurants and local markets that carry specialty items and/or a have gourmet or delicatessen section. The common thread shared by these venues is that they generally carry unique products of a caliber better than your large supermarket chains. Furthermore, their clients are well aware of and, in fact, anticipate the additional expense of quality products. Look for restaurants and small grocers that cater to clientele who will appreciate your custom-made treats and be willing to pay for a superior product.

When approaching these businesses, you will want to come prepared. A business presentation to a potential wholesale client is rarely conducted over the telephone. You should always call to schedule an appointment with the owner and/or purchaser. Occasionally, if a business owner knows about your products and has received requests for your cakes, they may be ready to place an order immediately. Your entire interaction with them may be by telephone with the contracts and payment flying through the mail.

More often than not, you will be meeting with new customers face-to-face. When setting the appointment for a presentation, ask if the business owner would like to be a "taste-tester." The owner or chef will be the ultimate arbiter of how good your products are. Usually a presentation is less about taste, however, and more about price and customer demand. You will need to convince owners that they should include your product in their menu or on their shelves.

When meeting a client, you want to present yourself and your business in the best possible light. For example, you would not dress as you would when baking or decorating your cakes! Your customers may be wearing sweats and sneakers, but you want to make the best possible first impression as a professional in the specialty food industry. You want to dress professionally, but not overdress. You are dealing with people who are self-employed just like you. Present yourself in a real, down-to-earth way.

Whenever possible, you should schedule presentations early in the week because weekends and the days leading up to the weekend may be busy with baking and delivery -- and you do not want to have to stop what you're doing to go on an appointment! Weekends also tend to be busier times for the entrepreneurs you are courting.

When presenting your products, you may wish to ask to sit at a table in a private office. You don't want to make your pitch in the store or workplace where the owner may be called away by ringing phones, customers and other distractions. Let the client know the meeting will be brief, as you both have plenty of work to do. Bring the following items with you: a wholesale price guide, a blank agreement(s), calendar, pen, and calculator. You should also provide the potential customer a sampling of your products. Don't try to bring too many samples. Many products can be seen in photographs. The samples you bring are simply to show a selection of your most popular products and the delicious quality of your work. Also, bring one or two unique items that a store owner probably has never considered.

Conduct the presentation assuming that the order will be closed and deposit received at this meeting. As your discussions progress, begin filling in the blanks on the agreement and discuss the cost of everything as you go along. You should offer discounts for larger quantities, and design a scale based on increasingly larger quantities. Be consistent with your pricing.

Once the decision to carry your products is made, it is very important to note the number of each item requested, as well as all special requests. Do not assume that you will remember-- write it down!

The presentation of your products in the store is a direct reflection of your business. You should be prepared to demonstrate your packaging for single items like cupcakes or cake pops as well as recommendations for presentation of cakes/slices. If you are so inclined, offer your services to prepare the display.

If your offer is accepted, this means that you may have to provide signage, a table or shelves, lifts for height variation, and other possible items to enhance and complete the presentation of your goods. Only offer to build a display if you are prepared to back it up with your time and materials. If the owner elects to have you build a display table(s), you may, of course, negotiate a fee for this.

Places to Sell Your Cakes

There are many places you can sell your cakes that offer additional opportunity to increase your brand awareness and revenues.

Gift & Tourist Shops: These are great businesses in which you may sell your products. Although the discount you provide to the shop owner means less profit than direct sales, you are opening the door to potential sales from repeat customers who will contact you directly, via your website, for example. Make sure your URL is included on your packaging.

Coffee Houses: Coffee Houses are common in both urban and rural areas. The clientele of these businesses are often looking for a product with quality above and beyond the norm. (Otherwise they would drink coffee made at home.) Your homemade cakes are a product that you could pitch to an independent coffee house that would set them apart from Starbucks and other chains.

Food Co-Ops: Independent, locally owned stores are very supportive of local sellers who are producing high-quality, unique products. You can supply a variety of cakes and may wish to focus on organic offerings here. Again, the patron of the local co-op is looking for high-quality products and is probably willing to pay more for all-natural items. Do you incorporate organic flour, sugar and/or perhaps locally sourced ingredients into your product line? If so, a food co-op may be a great place for you to sell.

Special Events Facilities: Introduce yourself to special event coordinators at country clubs, restaurants, churches, and other facilities that host weddings, rehearsal dinners, and other special events. Some facilities have no in-house food service and keep referral lists to share with their clients.

After an initial meeting with the contact person at such a facility, find out when his or her birthday is and deliver a box of cakes on their special day. You will be remembered and the referrals will probably become even more frequent and compelling!

Retail Sales: In addition to wholesale, wedding and occasion-cakes, you can sell in venues directly to the consumer. This method may require a great deal more work, as you will have to invest your time in locations outside of the home. Selling directly to the consumer has its advantages, however--namely, the increased profits. Here are a few ideas for meeting your consumers face-to-face.

Farmers' Markets: Outdoor and specialty farmers' markets are located in communities across the country. They draw a population of consumers looking for fresh, high-quality food and gift items. In most locations, there is only a small fee (or no fee) to participate in this kind of cooperative; you simply need to set up a booth or table with your products. In regions with multiple smaller towns within a half-hour to one-hour drive vicinity, you may be able to attend farmers' markets on different days of the week.

Fairs, Festivals & Kiosks: These venues may include summer festivals, Christmas craft fairs, autumn harvest days, etc. Each season and special event offers the potential for rapid sales as people are looking for unique gifts and impulse purchases. This is a great selling opportunity and can be a fun outing where you can meet long-term customers as well. Count on most of your sales at the event to be one-time-only purchases. However, you may garner follow-up sales if you provide a mailing list sign-up at your booth. Keep in mind that these events require fees to set up and participate. Ensure the financial investment is worthwhile. Most fairs and festivals keep this rate fairly low to accommodate home businesses such as crafters and farmers.

Fairs, Festivals & Kiosks also require a great deal of time and energy standing and greeting customers, and preparing and packing up your booth. How will you also take care of your regular customers? For specialized events or high-profile expos, such as a food expo or a restaurant show, you should determine if the investment in fees is appropriate to your business. These vendor opportunities can be expensive, starting at $500 to $1,000 for a small booth. Especially during your first year in business, you may wish to network with other vendors to determine if their participation in this type of event has resulted in sales for them.

If you decide to purchase a booth in a high-profile event such as a restaurant or wedding expo, you want to present your business professionally. Be prepared to be accessible to your customers all day or have some assistance in manning your booth. Leaving your booth to take a lunch or to go to the bathroom can result in lost sales. These events often have thousands of people circulating through them. The items you will want to have at a booth include: brochures, price lists, samples, business cards and--of course--products to taste. You may want to have plenty of samples to give away. When people taste your mouth-watering cakes, they will want to follow up or book you on the spot. Prepare packages with multiple quantities and varieties of your cakes.

10
LEGAL CONSIDERATIONS

When planning your cake business you must take the legal issues very seriously. For most people, the legal part of starting a food business can feel overwhelming and scary. Like so many other aspects of starting your cake business, the key is to research and compile checklists. This is certainly not the fun part of starting your business, but it is one of the most important. As you move toward your opening day, you will check off the required permits, paperwork, inspections, etc. Each state, county, and municipality will have its own regulations, permit and licensing requirements, and zoning restrictions. Do not avoid these issues, in hopes that they will not affect your business. Tackle the research head on.

No single book or website can prepare this information for you. The laws change from place to place and in some cases from street to street. To be a responsible business owner, you need to research the laws and guidelines where your business will be located and take seriously all the responsibilities that come with selling food to the public. Despite the variables, many of the requirements are universal and this chapter will address the legalities all cake businesses should consider. While the specifics will be up to your location and unique circumstances, this section will have you well on your way.

Many people mistakenly spend time and money planning a home-based cake business, only to discover the requirement of a commercial kitchen or a restrictive zoning ordinance. Never let your emotions rule your decision making process when it comes to regulations beyond your control. If you are planning a retail operation, you may discover that the lovely space you think would make an ideal bakery is actually more restrictive and costly to get up to code than another location the next town over.

This chapter will address the myriad of issues you will face in order to make your business legal. A significant portion will focus on the requirements for commercial bakeries out of the home, with a special section at the end for home-based cake businesses. Keep in mind that working within the law will create the foundation for your success, no matter the scale of your cake business. As a legal entity, you will have access to more venues and business opportunities. You will be able to document your success openly, enabling you to advertise. You will never fear being turned in to the health department from a competitor and you will always have a permanent record of your investment through tax records, profit and loss statements, etc., enabling you to sell the business for the maximum value when the time comes.

With your new business venture will come the legal costs of getting it off the ground. You will incur fees ranging from acquiring required licenses and permits to filing fees with the Secretary of State. These charges depend on the business structure you choose to set up and will vary from state to state.

In addition to a visit to your local SCORE office, a one-time consultation with an attorney should be obtained during your start-up process. This consultation can be used to develop necessary forms for the business, and provide advice on any further legal considerations needed. This research is part of any start-up. The fees can vary widely, but are typically tax deductible. Ask for referrals from other business owners or check with your Chamber of Commerce when searching for an attorney. You may also wish to call your local bar association because many have a referral service.

Some attorneys may charge a consultation fee of $50 to $500, but in most cases the fee will be applied to any services that you have them perform. The most common service that an attorney will provide is setting up the business type (corporation, LLC, sole proprietorship) that you choose and taking care of all the paperwork associated with keeping you legal.

Your attorney can also provide counsel on the liabilities involved in operating your cake business and attempt to insulate you from personal liability. In addition, you may want them to prepare service contracts tailored to your business so that you have recourse in the event that you don't get paid or a dispute arises with a vendor, client or employee.

Business Structure

When forming a business, you have several options. A sole proprietorship is a business in which you are the sole owner. This type of business can also be called a DBA or "Doing Business As" if you are using a business name rather than your personal name. Legally and for tax purposes, you are not separate from your business; rather you are operating under a different name. You are personally liable for your business and its debt; all income is added to your personal tax returns (pass-through taxation). If you are in the earliest stages of exploration, have no employees and are not selling anything, then this type of business is easy to setup, easy to maintain, and if you decide not to open a bakery after all, easy to dissolve. If your bakery moves beyond the planning stage, a sole proprietorship offers very little personal asset protection and is not advised.

The second business type is a partnership in which there is more than one business owner sharing in the profit and liability incurred by the company. A partnership, however, should be formed into a business that protects the partners involved, such as a corporation or limited liability company (LLC).

A corporation is a legal entity in which you (or you and your partners) would be members or shareholders. Through the formation of a corporation you will be insulated from personal liability that may occur in the operation of your business. However, keeping up the formalities of a corporation is a time consuming and expensive proposition. A corporation can buy real estate, enter into contracts, sue and be sued completely separate from its owners. Also, money can be raised easier via the sale of stock; its ownership can be transferred via the transfer of stock; and the tax advantages can be considerable (i.e., you are able to deduct many business expenses, healthcare programs, etc., that other legal entities cannot). If you are investing in something substantial enough to purchase real-estate, raise money by selling shares, and offer healthcare to your employees, then a corporation may be appropriate for you.

The most common choice for smaller businesses is the formation of an LLC -- Limited Liability Company. With an LLC you will enjoy the same protection from personal liability as you would in a corporation, but you do so without many of the formalities that are usually associated with a full-blown corporation. An LLC also provides easy management and "pass-through" taxation (profits and losses are added to the owner(s) personal tax returns) like a Sole Proprietorship/Partnership. There is an initial cost to establish your LLC and each state charges an annual fee to maintain it. In many states, you must also submit an "annual report" or "statement of information", which is a one-page form sent by the state. Some states also have a flat LLC tax that can range anywhere from $250 to the low thousands.

Organizational Documentation

If you determine that you will be creating an LLC, limited liability partnership, or corporation, there are some organizational documents you must file. The easiest way is to use an attorney or an online service such as Legal Zoom.

When you file your organizational documents, the agency (often the Secretary of State) will also check your business name to make sure it does not duplicate one being used by another business. To ensure your application is accepted and to save time, research first with the state filing office to make sure your business name is available. This can often be done online.

Keep in mind that a name may be available to use in your state, but you may have legal trouble if the name infringes upon the trademark of another business. Simply stated, you can't use a name (or logo, slogan, appearance, signage, or product name) that can be easily confused with a competing cake business or bakery that has registered that trademark.

Selecting a name that is not only available in your state, has an available URL, and has a very low likelihood of causing any customer confusion, takes time to research, but will avoid legal trouble down the road. Be mindful of national brands that have the legal war-chest to fight even the most far-fetched similarities. For example, in May 2010, Pillsbury's lawyers served a cease and desist notice to My Dough Girl, LLC a Salt Lake City, Utah Cake Retailer with one store. They claimed her use of the phrase Dough Girl infringed on their trademarked character, The Pillsbury Dough Boy. The owner changed her business name to RubySnap (rubysnap.com).

Business Name Registration

If you choose to present yourself under any name other than your proper legal name, you will have to register your fictitious business name. This is handled typically at the county level. First, conduct a search through the county database (usually online) to make sure the name is not already in use. Then, there is a simple form to fill out and a fee (anywhere from $10 to $100). Some states may have other requirements such as publishing the notification in a local newspaper classifieds. Your county clerk's office will provide the details about the process in your area.

Tax Considerations

As a business owner, you may be required to collect taxes on goods you sell. This is a complex matter that should be addressed by consulting your accountant. The tax laws that govern your business depend on the kinds of items you offer, how they are served, and how they are consumed. Moreover, they are frequently changing.

For example, in California, tax generally applies to sales of food and beverages if those items are served for consumption at your place of business. You are considered to have a place of business where customers consume their purchases if you provide tables and chairs or counters for dining, or provide trays, glasses, dishes, or other tableware; however, sales of hot bakery goods are not taxable when sold to go, unless they are sold as part of a combination package. You can see this is tricky! In just this one state's example, there are different rules based entirely on how the food is ordered and consumed.

By consulting an accountant, attorney, or even looking into your state and local requirements, you can determine whether there is a state sales tax or another type of tax that you must collect in the course of your business. Working with your local SCORE office is the best free way to explore your tax liability as they have assisted thousands of local entrepreneurs and know the ins and outs of your specific community. As a starting point, a complete listing of states' departments of revenue is listed at taxadmin.org/fta/link/.

Tax ID's

A federal ID number, called an FEIN or EIN is like your personal Social Security number, except it is for your business. Most businesses in the US are required to get an EIN. This number is used by the government to identify your business and you will use it over and over on many of your business documents. You need an EIN to open a business bank account, apply for business licenses, and to file a tax return. The name "employee identification number" is confusing because even if you don't have, or don't plan to have employees, EIN's are required for most businesses. The exception is if you are a sole proprietor without employees. Then, you can use your social security number as your identification. Partnerships, LLC's, and corporations need an EIN whether they have employees or not.

Obtaining an employer's ID number is as simple as using the IRS online form called "EIN Assistant". Once you complete the form, the number is assigned to you immediately and becomes part of your IRS record (for paying taxes) within two weeks. Note, LLC's must file their organizational documents before applying for an EIN.

Employment Tax

If you have employees, it is your responsibility to withhold taxes from their paycheck, keep track of the amounts you are withholding and make regular payments to the state and federal government. These taxes include federal income tax withholding, Social Security and Medicare taxes, and Federal Unemployment Tax Act (FUTA) taxes. http://tinyurl.com/bakery21

This may seem intimidating if you've never done it, but like anything else, it gets easier after a few times. Most entrepreneurs choose to manage this complexity by hiring a part-time bookkeeper and/or using an integrated bookkeeping/payroll software solution. Probably the best-known of these is Quickbooks. An accounting package simplifies the painstaking process of making calculations, completing reports, and writing and signing checks.

Tax Exemption

A seller's permit, also known as a Certificate of Authority or a Resale Certificate, exempts you from paying sales tax on some of your purchases including ingredients or anything that you resell. Handy when you buy items in bulk! Keep excellent records so the IRS doesn't think you're taking advantage of this benefit. The items you purchase without paying sales tax must be used solely for your business, not personal use. A state sales tax exemption can save you money by allowing you to purchase your products wholesale. Wholesale vendors usually require a copy of this certificate or the number in order to set up a wholesale account.

Most states provide the form online through the state tax department, but your local Chamber of Commerce should also have the information you need. However, once you've applied for a tax exemption certificate, you will be expected to start filing monthly or quarterly sales tax reports in most states.

Business Permits and Licensing

Business License

Just about all businesses -- home-based or retail -- need a county or city license. This is a general business license and is required in addition to a more specialized food production license for your cake business. The fees associated with getting a business license are typically minimal, if any. The best place to start is your local city hall or courthouse. See the city clerk, who should be able to direct you. You can also phone the city or county clerk's office with questions, or look in your local phone book under municipal government offices. Try a search online for "your city hall" on Google or Yahoo local searches to find the web site for your local city hall. A state business license may also be required. See the Addendum for each state's requirements.

Food Production License

Before you can start selling cakes to the public, you may be required to secure a food establishment permit from your state, county, or city health department. Typically, your local health department will be the source for this information. However, if you are operating under a cottage food ordinance, your state Department of Agriculture is the regulating body.

The cost of the permit is minor, while the preparation and expense to meet the requirements can be costly. Permits are required for permanent locations, as well as temporary operations such as a kiosk, mobile truck, or marketplace. If, for example, you bake cakes in a commercial kitchen to sell in a mobile vending business, both the kitchen and the truck will be inspected. If you rent a shared kitchen or space in a food incubator, you may be permitted to operate under their license. In fact, this is one of the key benefits to renting space in a commercial kitchen -- they meet all the health and safety requirements for your food business.

Health inspectors might seem intimidating to novice or unprepared business owners, but in fact, they are a great resource. While their job is ultimately to protect the community, in doing so, they protect you. Inspectors want to make sure that all areas of your food production meet the legal standards set by your community. Since most municipalities are burdened by layers of bureaucracy, the health inspector can help you traverse the red tape and give you the information about the requirements you'll have to meet whether you operate in home or out of the home.

In a health inspection, your inspector will be checking to see the cleanliness of the operation including utensils, equipment, and surfaces; how food is stored, prepared, and displayed; employee health and hygiene; the design and installation of equipment; organization of storage; cleanliness of restrooms; and the materials and construction of your overall space. The biggest concern of the health inspector is PHF or, potentially hazardous food. Potentially hazardous food is primarily defined in terms of whether or not it requires time/temperature control for safety to limit pathogen growth or toxin formation. For example, with cakes, consider the use of egg and dairy products and the potential of food borne illness resulting from inaccurate heating/cooling, cross contamination, packaging, storage, etc. Most states require at least one employee to have completed a food safety training course and be present at the time of inspection. You, as well as anyone working in your kitchen on a daily basis, should complete this course.

Prior to your opening day, you will be inspected. If your initial inspection results in any faults, you must correct them before the permit will be issued. Because a major problem could result in significant delay and expense, you should bring the health department into your planning process from the outset. For example, you don't want to invest in an opening day event only to find the grease trap you've installed is too small. Moreover, if you've been given a rent allowance from your landlord, you don't want any surprises that will delay your opening, and have to start paying rent without bringing in revenue. If you work with the health department from the outset in a spirit of cooperation most inspection faults (if any) will be minor.

Health departments will perform periodic inspections -- both scheduled and surprise -- on an on-going basis. The focus of these inspections is on critical risk violations, which are those violations most likely to contribute to food borne illness. Critical areas of focus will be safe food temperatures, employee practices such as hand washing, and an adequately supplied bathroom; the absence of vermin (immediate risks: rodents, cockroaches, flies); water and sanitation, including having enough hot water; the presence of a sewage disposal system. A sample inspection checklist and the bonus resource items are included on our website.

Re-inspections are performed as a follow-up to a routine inspection that results in written orders. Only violations not in compliance with the initial inspection will be shown on the re-inspection report. If all violations are in compliance at re-inspection, the report will state "no violations to report."

Once you've passed your first health inspection, teach your employees to operate your business in a manner that prioritizes health and safety. This will ensure that unannounced inspections are never an issue and that the public can be confident in patronizing your cake business.

Listed are a few things to keep in mind while you are being inspected:

Greet the inspector: Be calm, communicative, and remember that you are working with the inspector to keep your cake production process safe and customers healthy.

Do not refuse an inspection: Refusing an inspection creates an antagonistic relationship between you and the heath department for a long time. Rest assured that upon return with an inspection warrant you will be penalized for every infraction, no matter how minor.

Be friendly, but not overly social: Do not offer anything to your inspector, including food, coffee, water, etc. It is important to maintain a professional relationship with your health inspector and this is not a social call. More importantly, it can be seen as a bribe.

Walk and talk with the inspector: Accompanying the inspector shows your interest in food safety and allows you to know the details of any violation.

Take notes: This gives you something to reference when addressing violations or planning further employee training.

Ask questions: If you do not understand why something is a violation, ask. The inspector will explain what portion of the food code it violates and the proper solution. Try not to be confrontational, as it breaks down communication.

Do not take it personally: Nobody is perfect, and mistakes happen. Rather than dwelling on every violation the inspector finds, correct the mistakes and strive for a better inspection the next time around.

Fix critical violations on the spot: Critical violations are those directly related to food borne illnesses. If they are not corrected immediately, your customers can become sick. For violations that cannot be remedied on the spot, set a time frame for correction; the inspector will most likely perform a follow-up inspection for critical violations that require more time for correction.

Know your stuff: Inspectors often quiz managers and employees alike to gauge their knowledge of food safety and preparation processes. All owners and managers must have up-to-date training. In some counties, lack of food safety knowledge is a critical violation and can shut down a business.

Have records on hand: The inspector will ask for all of your records regarding food safety management. These can include temperature check records, receiving logs and employee illnesses. Also, the inspector will ask to see your operators permit to make sure it is current.

Something to remember: Part of a health inspector's job is education. If your facility is lacking in a specific area of safe food handling, arrange a date and time for the inspector to return and give your employees a food safety lesson. This will help ensure that your customers and employees have a healthy, enjoyable experience in your establishment.

In the Appendix of this book and on our website, you will find a list of contact information for each state's regulatory agency as well as a common checklist for health inspections. As a food service provider to your community, you should take your state's regulations; community's zoning regulations; and the liability aspects of owning a business very seriously. If you do not, you can face serious consequences, including fines, lawsuits, and the loss of your business.

The following is a list of standard equipment and conditions that are most often required from the heath department. When scouting locations, planning build-outs or second home kitchens, keep these items in mind as they may be unexpected expenses:

- 3-compartment sink with a grease trap installed
- Hand sink
- Low Radiation Lights that are covered
- Washable surfaces - walls, floors, cabinets, counter tops that do not retain flour, dirt, and dust
- Ceiling must be of non-absorbent material
- Separate refrigerator and freezer
- Storage for equipment - pans, spatulas, bowls, etc.
- Food safe storage for ingredients
- Adequate storage space for ingredients
- Approved water source

Insurance

This is probably the most important area of business ownership that is almost always overlooked at the outset. For those branching out from a home business, you may have simply been able to add an addendum, rider, or "endorsement" to your homeowner's policy, but when you step into the commercial side, having the right kind of insurance is vital.

General Liability Coverage: Liability insurance has several parts, all designed to protect you from loss when catastrophe strikes. The types of liability insurance you need to consider include, coverage for property damage, loss of use, personal injury, and special insurance that protects you against claims arising from raw materials you use in the creation of your cakes. You want to be protected from the unthinkable. Imagine your worst nightmare come true about your business, and you will understand the importance of liability insurance.

Consult with your attorney to determine the type of coverage you need, and don't be afraid to shop around. One warning: the cheapest insurance coverage is not always the best choice. You want coverage that comes with real protection, great service in case you have to file a claim, and an agent who can help you navigate the insurance industry successfully.

The standard liability coverage for a retail cake shop ranges from $1,000,000 to $5,000,000, depending on the size and scope of your business. Coverage should include product liability protection. For example, you use cherries as an ingredient in your cakes and the cherries are recalled. Even though your supplier and the manufacturer of the cherries are likely liable, a customer who gets sick eating your product can still sue or try to sue you, so having protection for product liability is critical.

Business Interruption Coverage: You should consider business interruption insurance and loss-of-use insurance, which protects you in the case that you are unable to continue using the location of your business because of damage from fire, flood, theft, vandalism, or closed roads. You can base your coverage on what you would need to survive (fixed costs plus income) for up to six months. Don't assume your coverage has everything you need; talk to your agent and read your policy carefully. Add coverage where you think you need it.

Property Coverage: This type of policy covers business personal property, including machinery, cooking equipment, ovens, point-of-sale systems, and stock. If you are renting, your landlord will likely require you to maintain a certain level of property insurance. Even if the lease indicates the landlord has a property insurance policy, you want to rely on your own individual insurance coverage. This will prevent litigation between you and the landlord, should there be a claim.

Workers Compensation: Workers' compensation benefits provide coverage for medical expenses, as well as reimbursement for lost wages when employees are injured on the job. Because some baking processes can be hazardous, it is more common for a bakery employee, than say, an office worker, to be injured on the job. The employers' liability portion of most Workers' Compensation policies protects your company in the event that an employee files suit claiming that your negligence was the cause of the work-related illness or injury. Workers' Compensation insurance is required in many states. There are multiple ways to purchase workers compensation, so it is best to consult your state for the regulations that affect you: http://tinyurl.com/bakery20

Equipment Breakdown and Miscellaneous Equipment Coverage: You should have insurance to cover your equipment as well (base it on the cost of replacing, not repairing, the equipment). This type of policy protects against damage caused by power surges, mechanical breakdown, motor burnout, and boiler damage. Some of the equipment in a commercial cake shop can cost five figures. You don't want to have to replace a vital 20-quart mixer or double convection oven without insurance.

Spoilage Coverage: One of the issues that bakeries face is food spoilage or food contamination as a result of equipment failure. Imagine the liability if a refrigerator full of cakes for a wedding broke down due to a power surge or motor burnout. While the Equipment Breakdown policy covers the refrigerator, it won't cover the food inside or the loss of income if you can't sell that product.

Other Policies to Ask Your Provider about: Business Auto Coverage

You need commercial auto coverage if you or your employees will use titled vehicles in their work. Examples include, making deliveries or picking up supplies.

Business Umbrella: An Umbrella Liability provides coverage for claims that exceed the amount of coverage on your General Liability policy. It may also add coverage to your Commercial Auto coverage as well as the Employers' Liability coverage on your Workers' Compensation policy. When claims are in excess of your other policies, this kicks in.

Business Crime Coverage: The primary crime for bakeries is employee theft of inventory. Other similar exposures may be present if retail and wholesale operations are conducted. Internet sales may create additional exposures such as identity theft or scam.

Home-Bakery

As mentioned above, this book will not attempt to list all the licenses, rules and regulations that apply to starting a home-based cake business, because they are always changing. Moreover, each government district has different requirements -- some more detailed than others. When researching your local rules and regulations, contacting the proper office in your area may take some perseverance. Particularly, if you choose to forgo the use of an attorney, you may be referred to several different offices until you find someone who can give you some useful advice.

When explaining your home business, be very specific about what your business is and what it is not. It may also make a difference if customers will be coming to your home to pick up products or if you will be delivering all of your cakes. If customers will pick up items, there may be health codes regarding the proximity of the food preparation area to the pick up or "reception" area.

Network with other home-based bakeries as well to find out how they operate their home-based business and how local authorities have dealt with them. Your local Chamber of Commerce is a good place to start looking for other home-based businesses.

Sales tax laws and amounts can vary from place to place as well. The sample agreement included in our resource section does not include tax in the payment section, but you should find out what is required in your area and include any required tax.

Investigate local zoning ordinances covering home-based businesses. Some residential neighborhoods have strict zoning restrictions that may prevent you from running a cake business out of your home. Yet, it may be possible to get a variance or conditional-use permit. Communicate with local governing authorities calmly and reasonably. If you can assure them that your cake business will not alter traffic patterns, that you are not opening a retail shop in your living room, and that you will not be hanging signage from your mailbox, etc. then you are likely to obtain a variance. Condominiums and planned communities may have bylaws that could affect your ability to do business out of your home.

Know the Law

Many factors should be considered if you decide to explore the possibilities of making foods other than cakes at home. It is possible that your town does not require a separate commercial kitchen for cake decorators, but does require separate facilities for other types of catering. Additional licenses, rules, and regulations may apply as well.

Many states allow "home-bakers" to operate without a state license or permit and/or may require a small fee. These are known as cottage food operations and more states are passing laws to permit them. While cottage food laws allow bakers to produce non-potentially hazardous foods, there are typically strict limits about where you can sell your cakes, how much you can earn each year, and how your cakes must be labeled. These laws are designed to help you test the waters, without the expense of a commercial kitchen, generate some income, and grow as a baker and business. However, there are limits to the amount of baked goods a home-bakery can produce. If you are serious about making a living in this business, then you will probably exceed that amount eventually. It is worthwhile to understand the state regulations, submit to periodic health inspections, complete food handler's certification, and bring your kitchen up to code if required.

When starting out you also need to secure the permission of local zoning commissions. Often local communities do not have ordinances in place for home bakery businesses and even with cottage food laws, may not have developed the governing rules. Operating within a cottage food structure exempts you from many of the health code documentation requirements that commercial bakeries must meet. However, you must operate as a business in all other ways. Record keeping is a large part of your legal responsibility:

- **Receipts for all business:** related expenses (ingredients, classes, etc.)
- **Mileage on Car:** running to the store for eggs, delivering cakes, developing cake pictures, and all things related to turning out those cakes
- **Utilities records:** gas and electricity that you use in baking and creating cakes should be deductible on your taxes. A percentage is usually used, depending on the volume of cakes and the size of your work area.
- **Cake order records:** Keep your cake order records for your protection and reference. If, for example, a wholesale restaurant client becomes irate because they ran out of your cakes during their dinner rush, he might try to hold you responsible. You can only furnish what they order. The order form will show him the amount of cakes that had been ordered. Protect yourself and keep those records for a sufficient period of time.

It is best to consult your tax advisor to determine how long you should hold onto records. An efficient way to do this is to scan your records and save them electronically -- remember to save your electronic files in more than one place to minimize the risk of losing them. These files work great as a reference when a new client wants to order cakes just like the ones she tasted at the restaurant more than a year ago. You may not remember what the restaurant ordered, but you can pull the order and you can find the flavor, design, and have all of the specifics in hand.

11
A CAKE SHOP

Location, Location, Location

Over time, if you are successful, your cakes will become "famous" in your community. People will drive for miles to experience your one-of-a-kind confection without hesitation. No other cake will do! Think about the foods and food establishments you love -- you might drive across town for a special ice-cream, pancakes, or frozen yogurt.

However, as a newcomer to the market, it is very rare for location to be secondary to product reputation. Your chances for success grow exponentially when your business is visible and accessible. If you decide to branch from a home-based operation to a store front, the first space you find will not necessarily be the best one for your business. That is because your emotional brain and the desire to announce your presence to the world can cloud your judgment. No matter how urgent your goals, never rush into a location if it isn't ideal. Often we try to convince ourselves that our concept is the one that will finally turn a vacant space into a success. Beware if the space has seen a string of business failures. While the price might seem great or the décor adorable, walk away. There is always another space that's even better than the first.

The closer you are to a community center, the more visible and accessible you will be. Bakeries, especially niche operations such as a cake shop, succeed when they are located in high traffic, visible locations with lots of residential families in the surrounding neighborhoods. Once again, the cake business is a volume business. If you are "going retail," then you need a large audience from which to draw customers.

The most important factor in choosing location is access. As you will read in the following case study, without good access, you simply cannot thrive no matter how great your cakes are. Never choose a location without trying to drive to it from multiple directions and analyzing the difficulties your customers might encounter.

Case Study

Company: Bakery Basket

Location: Boise, Idaho

Bakery Basket was a very popular bakery in West Boise. They marketed themselves as an old-fashioned bakery and offered seating for up to 90 eat-in guests. They served specialty coffees, in addition to their sweet treats, and offered a small but delicious selection of lunch sandwiches. The reviews of the bakery from customers were always four and five stars. Comments from customers included:

"Family owned, clean, and all is made fresh, not frozen products like others. Great sit down area, with good service."

"Bakery Basket has made many items for me to bring into work from pies, cakes and everything in between. Their products are fresh; the frosting is not that overly sweet gooey stuff you get at large chains; it is velvety soft and good. You pay a little more, but you also get better ingredients and to me it is well worth it. They are located in a good area of Boise. Stop in and try them!! You will not be disappointed."

Bakery Basket was a small, family-owned bakery that offered specialty temptations like eclairs and fresh muffins with a wide variety of donuts, bagels, and cakes. They offered special services like made-to-order birthday cakes with a special buttercream frosting recipe and also made wedding cakes. Though they were enormously popular, they made one bad decision that resulted in their going out of business after only a few years. They were in a location that was incredibly difficult to access.

In order to get to the parking lot, cars either had to cut through a gas station parking lot or go around a corner and turn in to a doctor's office parking lot and cut through the other side of the gas station. The bakery did not have its own direct access from the street.

Worse yet, the location was hidden behind other businesses with no visible signage from the road. The final straw appeared to be a median in the road that did not allow incoming traffic to turn left into the gas station and bakery.

It did not matter how delectable their products were or how inviting their dine-in area was. Not enough people were able to find them to continue generating enough revenue. Shortly after Bakery Basket went out of business, the entire area was torn out and reconstructed to be more accessible, but the median preventing left turns has still caused difficulty. Bakery Basket's story demonstrates the ultimate importance of location. You can do everything else right, but if you are in the wrong location, you add an uncontrollable risk component to your ability to stay in business.

Choosing Your Location

Often, aspiring business owners dream of owning a shop and scout locations they think would be ideal. Rather than waiting until space opens up in your coveted location, start doing an evaluation of the site's suitability now. Too often people make decisions based on emotion and ultimately choose a location for the wrong reasons.

Armed with comprehensive information such as demographic data, present and planned transportation routes, city and downtown land uses, municipal restrictions, and other related factors, you will be able to make a decision based on facts rather than assumptions.

When considering a site for your new shop, you must determine the market you seek and attempt to locate in a place most convenient to that population. Don't limit your imagination to a single location. Consider opportunities in the following settings:

- Residential areas
- Central trade areas
- Shopping centers
- Recreation areas
- Education facilities
- Other attractions

In addition to general areas for locating a cake business, you want to think more specifically about the neighborhood and the clientele you want to attract. Knowing the median income, ethnic make-up, site availability, competition, existing businesses, and growth patterns assures that you won't make an obvious mistake. While one kind of concept could thrive in one part of town, it could fail in another based on perceived price, authenticity, cultural relevance, and taste in another part of town. The Bureau of Census and the Department of Commerce provide detailed data on neighborhood make-up.

In some cases there are real-estate opportunities that are desired because of the long-established patterns of success, trendiness, or growth. In Saratoga Springs, New York for example, businesses long for storefront openings on Broadway Avenue.

Aspiring business owners must have the business plan to ensure that the return-on-investment of locating in a higher rent district will enable them to meet their obligations and make a profit. Some locations are so exclusive, or otherwise desirable, that retail space is not available or priced beyond the rate at which your business could be profitable. If no site is available or existing sites are priced too high, there is no alternative but to look elsewhere.

Conducting your own research will prepare you to make a sound selection. Traffic studies can be obtained from the broker managing the prospective building and, for less than $100, you can get a site demographic analysis online with a breakdown of the location you are contemplating and the income levels of the surrounding area. The following is a complete breakdown of variables to consider when selecting a location:

Locale

- Type of neighborhood: urban, suburban, etc.
- Customer profile criteria
- Other types of businesses in the neighborhood
- Pattern of growth
- New construction or remodeling underway

Appropriate Zoning and Codes

- Retail cake business/bakery specifically allowed
- Parking space(s) criteria
- Use permits
- Curb breaks
- Food service requirements

Competition

- Total number of bakeries
- Total number of stores selling similar and similarly priced items
- Total number of seats in each category
- Level of service
- New competition under construction or planned

Specific Lot Characteristics

- Clear title or lease considerations
- Adequate parking, square footage determined
- Landscaping and other features

Traffic Arteries

- Traffic counts
- Street patterns and flow direction

- Number of lanes
- Surface type and condition
- Curbs and sidewalks
- Type and quality of lighting
- Ingress/egress to site
- Obstacles and hazards
- Public transportation
- Distance(s) from intersections, transit, terminals, landmarks

Utilities and Municipal Services

- Electricity
- Gas
- Other energy source(s)
- Water
- Sewers
- Police protection
- Fire protection
- Hydrant(s) existing or proposed
- Trash collection
- High speed internet

Visibility

- Driving
- Walking
- Degree of obstruction
- Sign location and height

Cost Data

- Cost per square foot
- Site Improvement cost(s)
- Taxes

When you've identified a few locations that seem likely to work for you, it's a good idea to spend time "stalking" each location. Become familiar with the type of clientele the location draws. Look at the parking lot. Walk through the existing shops as a customer. See if your vision of your business fits with the feel of the location.

Contact the broker or landlord to see the inside of your potential space. Make note of things like plumbing and electrical (for most large ovens you will need to have a site equipped to handle 220 volts). How much effort will be involved in making the location ready for your business? Will the space be large enough to accommodate growth? Is there enough storage? Is there a dedicated delivery area?

If you are considering a retail operation in a shopping center location, there is no doubt that a sidewalk-accessible space is often the most ideal location. Consistent foot-traffic is important to a steady sales flow.

You should also consider the visibility factors of the location. Is your building visible from the street? Will traffic be able to see your store sign? Does the shopping center offer additional center post signage for added visibility?

Zoning Codes

Before leasing a site, take the time to check with the municipality's planning and zoning commission, or whoever controls land use, to insure that your prospective business can be opened. Because entrepreneurs often envision our community differently than our local governments, we often see opportunity in places that are not (but could be) zoned for food establishments.

A common example of this type of restriction that is a local ordinance that requires a minimum number of off-street parking places for all food establishments regardless of size. Parking is just one example of the many restrictions that prevent or seriously delay the opening of a brick-and-mortar shop. Sign codes, use permits, building and lot requirements, and curb breaks must be explored before signing a lease.

Once you have narrowed down your location prospects, you can proceed to other considerations like landlords, leases, and costs.

What Makes a Good Landlord?

The best way to determine whether or not a landlord is going to meet your needs is to talk to the other tenants. You'll likely hear all the horror stories. They'll fill your ear with all the gossip, but you'll also find out if the landlord is pretty good at getting repairs done and keeping the lot clean while not gouging you on lease renewals.

In addition to talking to the tenants, you can check with the Better Business Bureau and push the leasing agent to allow you the opportunity to speak directly with the landlord if you have additional questions.

Some things you may want to consider asking the landlord:

1.Is there a tenant association?

2.Do you have promos that you pay for like sidewalk sales?

3.Since in most situations the first two answers will be no, the next question may be if you can organize your own promotional opportunities for the shopping site.

4.Ask about conditions at different times of year. Are there snow removal problems? Vandalism issues? Special security requirements?

Be sure to shop carefully for your location because you'll often be obligated to the location for at least the minimum lease term (two years or more), whether you are able to stay in business or not.

Lease Negotiations

When you are negotiating your lease, there are several things you need to understand. How much leverage you have in the negotiating process depends on how desperate the landlord is to get a tenant. If you are opening your business in a community or location where there are several other people wanting the same spot, your landlord will have the upper hand. If, however, you are after a spot that has been sitting empty or you have five other locations you can choose from, you are in a great position to bargain.

Before beginning the negotiations, you should check with the trade association (such as the American Bakers Association, americanbakers.org) about the industry standard for lease costs as a percentage of income. For example, if the gross income is $200,000 per year, and the industry standard is 13%, your total occupancy costs should be no more than $26,000 per year. (Of course this will vary based on location, so check your Chamber of Commerce for local adjustments of this variable.)

Remember, occupancy costs include both the rent portion of your lease, plus additional costs like your percentage of utilities, insurance, and maintenance. When negotiating the lease with a landlord, you should not be willing to exceed the industry standard.

Tenant Finish Allowance

Another consideration, and possibly the most important consideration if you are converting an existing building that has not served as a bakery before, is the tenant finish allowance. When negotiating your lease, this is a concession that should be given by the landlord for remaking the building to be used for your business. It is usually negotiated in dollar per square foot. For example, if your landlord offers you $10 per square foot and you are leasing 1,500 square feet, you would have $15,000 to finish the space and make it ready to use for your business.

In most cases, the landlord actually has funds set aside for this purpose and can pay your contractors directly, limiting the amount of cash you have to have available to get started. However, there are certain items like the oven or HVAC system that the landlord will not cover in the tenant finish allowance.

You should be able to negotiate upgraded air conditioning, new flooring and counters, the removal of all the items being torn out, and other appearance improvements. If your landlord is not able to offer a tenant finish allowance, you may be able to negotiate free rent for the first two to four months in exchange for making the improvements yourself.

Lease Term

Unless you are an established business with a good business credit history, do not expect the lease term to be longer than a few years. The landlord will be taking a greater risk on you as a new business and will therefore keep the term shorter and charge you more in rent than the anchor store would be charged per square foot (anchor stores are not profitable for landlords, but strip malls and shopping centers simply cannot survive without them).

If you go out of business before the lease is up, you still have to pay the lease, and the landlord has a lien against your property in the building as security.

Personal Guarantee

If the landlord requires you to sign a personal guarantee for the lease, this makes it possible for the landlord to go after your personal assets if the business closes. You should try to avoid this if possible, but if you choose to sign a personal guarantee, limit the liability, for example, to stocks and bonds, but not your personal home or bank account. This is an unusual situation and should be a last resort, for example, if the space is in great demand. Otherwise, there are usually other location opportunities that do not put your personal finances in jeopardy.

Bargaining Points

Try to get your landlord to agree to limit the amount of increases when you renew your lease. In some cases, you can pin the increase to economic conditions or revenue. Escalations are often tied to a known method of calculation, such as cost-of-living index.

You can also negotiate a discount on rent if you can pay a few months at once, such as paying three months' rent up-front and getting one month free.

Options

When negotiating your lease, get plenty of options from your landlord (to renew the lease) to ensure you have the space available if you need it. Longer-term leases are cheaper, but difficult to get when you are newly established and have no credit. Be prepared for your options to come with a market adjustment for the cost of the lease, but try to negotiate the lowest possible terms you can.

Costs to Consider Beyond the Lease

When opening a cake business, you need to be aware of the many additional costs to consider beyond the lease. It usually takes about three times as much cash to open a business as people expect it to take. It is important to do your homework and know how much you are going to need. There are loans available through the Small Business Association that can help.

Signage

A good sign promoting your business and adding visibility is crucial to your success. Signs can cost $5-$10,000, so budget early for this necessary cost. While it's not often, you might be able to negotiate the cost of the sign as a concession from your landlord.

The Grease Trap

Grease traps are expensive to install and difficult to manage. Ideally, you will find a location where the landlord already has a grease trap, which would make the location advantageous. If you have to install a grease trap, it can be an expensive start-up cost, about $10,000, to install.

CAM

"CAM" stands for common area maintenance, which includes some shared utilities, landscaping, maintenance, and other costs. This cost will be in addition to your lease amount each month, so be sure you talk to the landlord about the cost and budget for it.

Deposits

If you set up new utilities, such as a new phone line for your business or you lease credit card processing equipment, a deposit will be required.

Leasing Checklist

Leasing a commercial space instead of purchasing commercial real estate is a smart move for a cake business with no track record. While your confidence is high, you must be realistic that there is a chance for failure. Buying a building is a potentially far greater risk than leasing. Unfortunately, there are fewer tenant protections and no standard lease agreements. You'll need a lawyer's help to negotiate the best deal on a commercial lease.

Every commercial lease should be in writing and should include the following details:

The rent: Include any increases (called escalations). You'll want to know the going rate for space in the neighborhood before you begin negotiating. It also helps to let the landlord make the first offer, and ask for a lower rent than you think you can initially get. When there is an economic downturn and businesses are closing, leases obviously drop. Accordingly, when there is a surge in demand for desirable locations, rents rise.

The term: How long the lease runs, when it begins, and under what conditions you can renew the lease. A shorter lease means less commitment, but less predictability for the long run and potentially higher rents. Since location is very important for a cake business, you may want to opt for a longer lease. You can always attempt to renegotiate lower rents or improvements as time goes on.

Utilities: Whether your rent includes utilities, such as phone, electricity, and water, or whether you'll be charged for these items separately.

Fees: Whether you'll be responsible for paying any of the landlord's maintenance expenses, property taxes, or insurance costs, and if so, how they'll be calculated.

Deposits: Any required deposit and whether you can use a letter of credit instead of cash.

Description: A description of the space you're renting, square footage, available parking, and other amenities.

Build Out/Improvements: A detailed listing of any improvements the landlord will make to the space before you move in. Your landlord may be more willing to make lots of expensive improvements if you're signing a longer lease.

Representations: Any representations made to you by the landlord or leasing agent, such as amount of foot traffic, average utility costs, restrictions on the landlord renting to competitors (such as in a shopping mall), compliance with Americans With Disabilities Act requirements, and so forth. These may come in handy later when you want to renegotiate your lease.

Assurances: That the space is zoned appropriately for a cake business/bakery. Of course, you'll also want to verify this information with local zoning authorities.

Sublease: Whether you'll be able to sublease or assign the lease to someone else, and if so, under what conditions. You'll want to negotiate the ability to sublease so that you can move with as little financial pain as possible.

Termination: How either you or the landlord can terminate the lease and the consequences.

When it is time to renegotiate your commercial lease, you'll want to document your reasons for a lower rent or more space improvements with hard facts regarding lower foot traffic than represented, a downturn in your industry, and so forth. Some landlords will even be willing to take a percentage of your sales instead of a flat rental fee when economic times are slow.

As a tenant, you have far more leeway when negotiating a commercial lease rather than with a residential lease, which is one reason why having your own lawyer to represent you in negotiations is so important. A lawyer can also research zoning laws and local ordinances and educate you on the local real estate market conditions and customs.

12
FOOD SAFETY

To be successful in any food related business, one must produce items that are safe and wholesome. The production of safe foods is your responsibility. Time and temperature abuse of foods contaminated with food-borne pathogens will certainly lead to a food-borne outbreak that will likely destroy your reputation and business. If anyone gets sick after eating your cakes, you may also find doctor bills or worse, a lawsuit on your hands. While this is the reason you have liability insurance, your reputation is far more difficult to recover. These problems can be avoided if you follow safe food handling practices. Be obsessive about food safety! While the incidents are rare, they do happen and can be devastating.

Most jurisdictions require that you have a Food Manager's Certificate to make food for public consumption. This might also be called a Food Safety or Food Sanitation permit. The regulating health agency in your community wants to make sure you're educated in proper sanitary practices.

An example of a food safety program is ServSafe, offered by the National Restaurant Association Educational Foundation, which provides state-by-state regulations and guidance. You can visit their website at servsafe.com/Foodsafety/. Another helpful organization for food safety is the American Bakers Association (americanbakers.org). According to the ABA, extra attention needs to be paid to food defenses, allergen controls, and sanitation. Because of the Bioterrorism Act, there are regulations that govern how vigilant you must be about your ingredient sources.

Even though smaller bakeries and cake shops are not required to maintain the same level of security as a wholesale distributor, developing clear food safety policies can protect you from risk and reduce the likelihood of introducing any kind of contaminants to your customers.

A food safety issue that needs to be clearly addressed is the control of allergens. Having good cleaning and sanitation processes that help to remove allergens from equipment can reduce risk. In addition to maintaining good sanitation habits, you should offer any employees regular monthly training on food safety and sanitation issues. Offer incentives to your employees for completing food safety training and make regular safety presentations part of your business culture.

When developing policies regarding food safety issues, address the following:

- Store potentially hazardous foods, such as eggs and milk, in the refrigerator immediately (33 to 40°F).
- Purchase high-quality foods from a reliable vendor. The food should be in good condition with the packaging intact, fresh (not beyond expiration date), and at the proper temperature.
- Dry staples should be stored at 50 to 70°F.
- Practice First-in-First-Out (FIFO) to insure safety and quality of your items.
- Ideally, frozen foods should be thawed in the refrigerator 18 to 24 hours prior to preparation. However, thawing under cold running water (<70°F), in the microwave, or extending the cooking time are all acceptable methods for thawing food.
- Practice good personal hygiene when preparing and handling food. Wash hands before food preparation, after handling raw foods, after using the restroom or any time hands become soiled.
- Take measures to prevent cross-contamination if you cook any other foods in the same space where you bake and decorate cakes.
- Clean and sanitize food contact surfaces such as counter tops, cutting boards, equipment and utensils. One tablespoon of bleach per gallon of water is an effective sanitizing agent.
- Wash fresh fruit thoroughly under cold running water. In refrigerator storage, make sure fresh fruits are wrapped or stored in containers.
- Wear clean clothes and aprons when preparing food.
- Do not use the same towel to wipe food contact surfaces that you use for wiping hands.
- Clean storage and kitchen areas regularly.
- Practice good housekeeping and implement a pest control program for eliminating the spread of disease.

HACCP

Hazard Analysis and Critical Control Point (HACCP) is a food safety approach that can help you develop policies and procedures that address the physical, chemical, and biological hazards that can affect the safety and quality of your food. The focus of an HACCP protocol is on developing prevention measures rather than reactionary measures for food safety.

HACCP is an internationally recognized food safety protocol. Because food borne illness is something that can significantly harm your clientele, even though smaller bakeries are not required to have HACCP procedures, the additional focus you place on preventing unsafe food handling practices from occurring, the better you mitigate your risk as a business owner.

The National Restaurant Association has estimated that a single incident of food poisoning can cost your business $75,000. For many small cake shops, one incident could cost enough to damage your business seriously. To make it easier to develop an effective food safety management program, the state of Alaska has developed a free Active Managerial Control program at dec.state.ak.us/eh/fss/amc/amcbroch.htm that you can download. This interactive program can help you develop your food safety protocols by creating customizable Standard Operating Procedures and checklists. A solid HACCP protocol will include the requirement of a Certified Food Protection Manager, ample food safety training for all employees, written and well-maintained SOPs, and ongoing monitoring and correction of your food safety system.

13
EXPENSES

Whether you are a home-based baker or starting a retail cake shop, there are several expenses you need to anticipate. One of the biggest mistakes new business owners make is not planning wisely for the amount of capital needed, which is typically at least twice what you think it will be.

Research Costs

Research is an important component in developing your cake business. You've already invested in research with the purchase of this book. Basic business costs can be researched online at costhelper.com. Any books you purchase or courses you take are also part of your research costs. Keep all receipts, including automobile expenses, as you will probably be driving to research your competition, conducting traffic pattern surveys, checking out perspective locations, etc.

Working Capital

It is important to have cash on hand to run your young business. This includes cash to buy supplies, provide change, petty cash, and any unforeseen expenses that are sure to crop up from time to time.

Advertising

It goes without saying that there will be costs to promote your new business. Advertising may include the costs associated with building a website, placing a Yellow Pages ad, signage, paid listings, newspaper ads, and more. Additionally, there are the costs associated with any promotions you may conduct in the first few weeks or months of your business, such as discounts.

Legal Fees and Insurance

Consulting an attorney is important in starting your business. There will be costs associated with legal advice such as setting up a legal business entity, reviewing your contracts, registering your business name, etc. Adequate insurance, like liability protection, is another unexpected expense in starting a business that you can't afford to be without.

Labor

While you may not have many employees at first, you are likely to need short-term labor for any work – renovation, sign installation, painting, electrical, plumbing, etc. – required to get up and running.

Licenses and Permits

Licensing costs range from location to location and run from small amounts to hundreds of dollars per year. Make sure you budget for these expenses.

Slush Fund

You should have enough money to run your business for several months, taking into account all of the operating expenses upfront. This is a safety net that most businesses fail to think about and is ultimately the reason they close.

When first starting, you really don't know the ebb and flow of sales and expenses. Depending on when you start your business, sales may be explosive, but then experience a natural plateau. For example, you may have big sales during the holidays followed by slower sales in January. Having the cash to stay afloat during slow times is the difference between success and failure. In addition to bakery equipment, you will need phone service, a dedicated phone line for processing credit cards, internet service, front end displays, a cash register, and other business equipment. Most importantly, you may have an unexpected expense such as a major repair or an insurance deductible.

Equipment

It's best to start with the least amount of equipment possible and to add only what you need, as you need it. Be frugal and careful. Keep all equipment maintained to prolong its life. Be sure to shop wisely and reserve your capital expenditures for the most important piece of equipment: your oven.

If you are operating a home-based cake business and plan to create a product with your existing kitchen equipment, make sure your planning is consistent with this constraint. Create a product line-up that will work well in the space you have and with the scale of a home kitchen. You probably won't have a multi-deck oven or a walk-in refrigerator in your home (and in accordance with certain licenses, you legally may not be permitted to) so you need to calculate your production capacity accordingly.

Supplies and Equipment for a Retail Operation (commercial cake business)

(This will vary depending on the scale of your cake business. While it is geared toward a retail operation, many of these supplies are necessary and useful for a home business as well. See the following section for the home-based equipment basics.)

Baking Supplies

- Greaseproof paper
- Tissue paper
- Foil
- Icing scraper or comb
- Icing ruler or comb
- Serrated knife

Kitchen Equipment – Prepping, Baking & Cooking

- Double stack oven(s)
- Range top
- Countertop Mixer
- Blender
- Food Processor
- Loader
- 20 quart Hobart mixer
- Refrigerated display case
- Double door commercial refrigerators
- Microwave
- Scale
- Cake Pans
- Sheet Pans
- Oven Peels
- Gm/Oz Scale
- Saucepans
- Knives
- Timer
- Oven Thermometer
- Whisks
- Thermometers
- Wooden Spoons
- Measuring Cups
- Oven Mitts
- Sieve
- Dough Scrapers
- Ladles
- Pastry Brushes
- Sifter
- Measuring spoons

Beverage Supplies

- Coffee Maker
- Coffee Pots
- Coffee Mill
- Cappuccino Maker
- Coffee Syrups

- Juicer
- Espresso Machine
- Ice Machine
- Water filtering system

Kitchen Equipment – Storage

- Reach-in refrigerator unit (prep)
- Single unit line refrigeration
- Double unit line refrigeration
- Walk in refrigerator and freezer
- Upright freezer
- Counter Freezer
- Chest Freezer
- Cooling Racks
- Flour Bins
- Baskets
- Dough Tubs
- Shelving

Kitchen Equipment – Cleanup

- Triple sink
- Garbage Disposal
- Handsink
- Dishwasher
- Hand wash single sink
- Prep sinks
- Grey water sink

Dining Room

- Tables
- Chairs
- Bar stools
- Menus
- Menu Board
- Tablecloths
- Lamps, lighting
- Self-service counter for coffee prep
- Bookshelf/newsrack
- Music system, stereo

Office Equipment

- Computer
- Desk
- ChairPrinter
- File Cabinet
- Cash Register
- Register Tape
- Letterhead and envelopes
- Purchase orders
- Receipt Pads
- File Folders
- Counter
- Telephone
- Fax

Cleaning Supplies

- Garbage cans
- Mop and Bucket
- Mopheads
- Brooms
- Dustpans

Bleach

Handsoap

Floorsoap

Kitchen Soap

Garbage Bags

Miscellaneous Supplies

Dishes-plates, saucers, etc.

Glasses, coffee cups

Flatware

Paper Bags

Boxes –cakes to go

Plastic wrap

Aluminum foil

Paper cups

Napkins

Receiving

200 lb. receiving scale

box knife

(2) dunnage rack 36"

Storage

Dry storage

(2) #10 can racks

(4) wire shelving w/post

(4) dunnage rack 36 inch

(6) 36 gallon ingredient bin w/slidecover

(6) polycarbonate food box

18 X 26 X 15 inch

(6) polycarbonate food box

18 X 26 X 9 inch

(6) polycarbonate food box - 18 X 26 X 6 inch

(6)polycarbonate food box - 18 X 26 X 3 inch

(54)polycarbonate food box cover 18 X 26

(12)polycarbonate food box - 12 X 18 X 9 inch

(12)polycarbonate food box cover 12 X 18

(6) 12 quart round containers w/lid

Cold storage

(1) refrigerator thermometer

(4 sections)wire shelving w/post

(4) dunnage racks 36 inch

(6) polycarbonate food box - 18 X 26 X 15 inch

(24)polycarbonate food box - 18 X 26 X 9 inch

(6) drain trays for food boxes - 18 X 26 inch

(6)polycarbonate food box - 12 X 18 X 9 inch

(12)polycarbonate food box - 12 X 18 X 6 inch

(18) polycarbonate food box cover 12 X 18

(6) 12 quart round containers w/lid

(6) 8 quart round storage container w/lid

(6) 3.5 quart round storage container w/ lid

(6) 2 quart round storage container w/lid

(1) 28 gallon lettuce container w/dolly

Bake Preparation

(4 sets)measuring spoons

(1 set) dry measures

(4) 1 cup measure

(2) 24 ounce aluminum scoop

(2) 32 ounce aluminum scoop

(2) 84 ounce aluminum scoop

(1) dough scale

(1) 24 inch french whip

(2) 18 inch french whip

Utensils

13 inch serving spoons solid

13 inch serving spoons slotted

12 inch spring tongs

9.5 inch spring tongs

Bus Station/Ware Washing

(2) dishwashers aprons

(1) maximum hold thermometer

(18)plate/tray racks

(10) flatware washing baskets

(4) all purpose racks

(2) 20 inch pot brush

(2) 8 inch pot brush

(2) bake pan brush

(12) stainless metal sponges

(12) green pads

General Cleaning Supply

Hand and nail brushes

(2)Hi-Lo brushes w/squeegee

(1) drain brush

(1) steam kettle brush

(2) coffee urn brushes

(1) stack oven brush

(4) heavy duty hand brush

(12) 16 ounce spray bottle

(144) hand towels

(2) mop buckets and wringer

(2) mops

(2) wet floor signs

(1) counter brush

(2) floor brooms

(6) 28 gallon grey trash can w/lids

(3) dollies for 28 gallon trash can

(4) rectangular trash cans

Equipment Recommendations for a Home Business

A home-based cake business can get started with a modest set of equipment. Most home businesses start by using the appliances and tools they already own. They focus on making products based on the equipment already available to them and wait to expand when cash flow enables them to do so. The above list is fairly comprehensive; the small home-based cake business can get by with much less. You will need the following if you don't already have them:

Sufficient counter space: Just as with your family baking, a cake business can never have enough counter space. As mentioned previously, a rolling cart is a great way to add additional counter space. Alternatively, consider adding a folding table or table on wheels to provide additional space

An oven: This does not have to be a professional baking oven, although it should regulate the temperature correctly. An oven thermometer is a good investment in case you need to adjust the temperature. If your oven is under-cooking in one corner and burning in another, it may be time to head to the appliance store.

Stand-up electric mixer: This is an essential piece of equipment that you should acquire immediately if you do not already own one. A stand-up mixer allows you to multi-task and is a huge time saver. Furthermore, hand mixers can't handle the workload and will burn up their motors very quickly under the strain. Treat this critical piece of equipment with great care and never overtax it.

Refrigerator: Your cake business will require a sizable refrigerator. When evaluating refrigerator space, keep in mind the competition between your family needs and your business needs. If it is within your budget, purchase a second refrigerator for your cake business.

Baking sheets: Consider investing in professional non-stick sheets.

Cooling racks: Start with two cooling racks at least 12" wide. Purchase larger racks as your business requires.

Piping (or pastry) bags for icing: We like to buy professional pastry bags in bulk from a cake business supplier such as Bakery Crafts (www.bakerycrafts.com).

Couviers: For changing tips easily. Efficiency is the key to keeping your hourly rate profitable; therefore, you don't want to waste time swapping out pastry tips.

Tips: Basic tips. Purchase others as needed.

Dishwasher, Cake-cutters and Bowls

A Note About Your Electric Mixer

Your electric stand-up mixer will be the workhorse of your kitchen as you begin mixing cake dough and icings. Besides your oven, the mixer is your most valuable piece of equipment. Invest in the best one you can afford and make sure it has regular maintenance when necessary.

Purchasing Cake Sheets

When purchasing cake sheets, it is advisable to shop at a professional bakery equipment supply house, craft store, or online baking site, rather than a department store. Notice the difference in quality and price. If you plan on using your sheets for a long time, investing in a quality product makes all the difference. It's a good idea to purchase multiple sets of sheets because the speed of your work flow is greatly enhanced if you don't have to stop, wash and refill a sheet. As your business grows, you will want even more sheets, but try to purchase sheets based on your average quantity.

Buying Used Equipment

You can often save a significant amount of money by purchasing your equipment used. Just as with car buying, however, there are pros and cons to buying used. For example, you should be cautious when buying refrigeration equipment used, as repair costs can quickly add up. You may end up spending more money than if you had just bought it new.

A second down side to buying used equipment is that it will not include the warranties typically included in a new purchase. Used equipment from auctions, closed businesses and eBay/Craigslist, etc. are almost always sold "as is." Meaning, as soon as it breaks down, the cost to repair is your responsibility. The good news is that many pieces of bakery equipment are nearly indestructible. If one small part goes, you can contact the manufacturer for a replacement part. Keep in mind, this requires a bit of extra effort on your part tracking down parts. Certain items, such as mixers, are better suited to buy used because they are known to work properly for a long time.

There are several auction sites where you can shop for used professional equipment like eBay, and Craigslist, but you should also check local auctions and closing restaurants in the region. Auctionzip.com is the easiest way to find local auctions that include restaurant/bakery inventory.

Equipment as an Investment

When you are really ready to make a go of your business, you need to determine exactly what you can afford to invest. With a pool of available funds specifically earmarked for your new business, you will probably have to do some shopping. Typically, the biggest investments you will need to make are your oven, refrigeration and electric mixer. Once you complete your research and purchase equipment, keep in mind that there are a host of other wonderful items that could be used in your cake business. If you are one of those people who enjoy shopping and new technologies, be wary of going too far, too fast–to purchase more than you really need. You see, despite all of the wonderful products that are out there, most of your work will be done with a few essential tools. Be steadfast about buying only the tools required for the cakes you are offering. This means planning ahead and making design and recipe decisions early on. (You can always change your mind.) Unless a special request comes in from a customer for a custom design, you really won't need anything other than the basics listed earlier. When you receive unusual requests, you simply make a special purchase and pass along part of that cost to your client.

14
MANAGING YOUR BUSINESS

Because there is so much to keep track of in any business, we recommend hiring an accountant to set up a few essential systems to keep you organized.

Paperwork: Don't fall into the trap of relying on electronic records to organize your files. Keep paper versions of everything in case you are audited or need to reference a contract. Financial documents need to be kept for seven years.

Accounting: Have your accountant set up an invoicing system for all of your cake orders and events. Set up a system for paying bills, reconciling deposits, managing petty cash, and paying taxes. Learn how to use these systems and keep them simple.

Cash Management: If you are opening a physical location, you will need a system to manage cash. There are two options: Cash Registers and Point of Sales Systems.

Cash Registers: If you've ever worked in retail, you've probably run a cash register. If not, consider that the cash register has been around a long time, and for good reason. They are sturdy, easy to operate (once you learn), and while not particularly high tech, they provide a good account of your daily sales.

Point of Sales Systems (POS): A POS is like a cash register on steroids, with an integrated computer, monitor, cash drawer, receipt printer, customer display debit/credit card reader, and often a barcode scanner.reader. This may be overkill for your needs. However, new innovations with the ipad/tablet may be something to consider. The Square Register, for example, can be integrated with a cash drawer and receipt printer. https://squareup.com/register

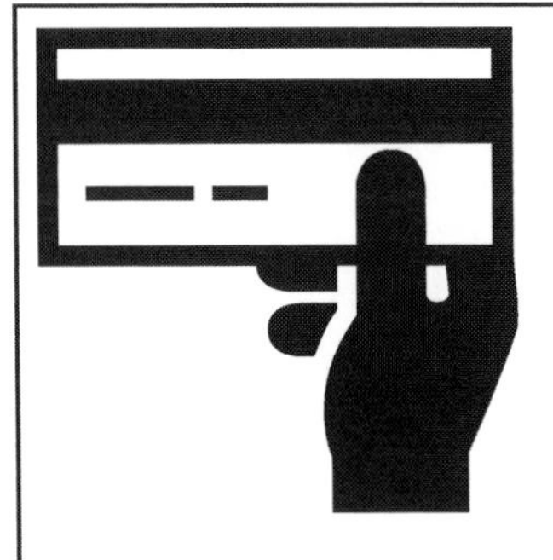

Accepting Credit Cards

Accepting credit cards is a convenience most professional businesses offer. The main benefit is that when a client wants to book a date, you can take the non-refundable deposit right over the phone (unlike a check that you must wait for). The downside is the expense and fees associated with every transaction. There is a wide range of services available, so do some investigation. Ask other businesses who they use. You'll want to compare rates and fees. Here are a few of the most common options available to small business owners:

Paypal: Paypal Virtual Terminal has a monthly fee of $30 plus a fee per transaction. Customers can order by phone, fax, or mail with debit or credit card.

Square: Square is a physical credit card reader that attaches to your iOS or Android device enabling you to swipe the card or type in the card manually. No monthly or startup fees, transaction fees only. The only downside is that Square places a hold on phone-in transactions over $1000 (monthly limit).

Google Merchant: Google Merchant enables you to invoice your client via email for credit/debit card purchase.Per transaction fees only.

Intuit GoPayment: Like Square (and others) GoPayment uses a physical reader with a smartphone and only charges per transaction.

POS Systems. There are several point of sale systems designed specifically for bakeries and small business such as Bakesmart [http://www.bakesmart.net/] and Shopkeep, [http://www.shopkeep.com/] These systems will integrate with a traditional merchant service provider such as Authorize.net [http://www.authorize.net/]

Potential costs include: software charges, support fees, hardware (computer, ipad, etc.), and transaction charges.

The Concept of Cash Flow

Cash flow is simply the movement of money in and out of your cake business. Cash comes in from the sale of your products and services and goes out for the cost of your expenses like labor, ingredients, and rent. One of the biggest problems facing business owners is maintaining adequate cash flow. Without enough cash, a business will not remain viable. Understanding and managing your business's cash flow is crucial to your success.

Prepare Your Profit and Loss Statement

Remember all of the work you did to create your business plan? Part of that process was developing financial statements, including a profit and loss statement. As a start-up business, your profit and loss statement is based on estimates; but once you open your business, you can use your accounting software to create actual profit and loss statements. In the Resources section of our website, cake-business.com, we have provided a spreadsheet for you to prepare your profit and loss statement.

You should complete your profit and loss statement before preparing your cash flow statement. Use your cash flow statement as a tool to help you control costs. Unlike other statements, this financial report helps you understand how much cash is coming in and out of your business for a given period.

Managing Employees

Managing employees effectively starts before you hire them; before you hire an employee, you should have a clear idea of what you need from him or her. This expense is a large draw from your profits, so make sure the money is well spent.

Are you hiring someone who will eventually take over some of the management duties, such as running the front counter (sales), or are you hiring someone who will take over some of the lower-end duties such as cleaning and repetitive decorating? Describing what you need in an employee should ultimately take the form of a clear and concise job description that identifies the education level and skills needed with an outline of the job duties to be performed. With a clear description, you will be more effective in advertising for, interviewing, and choosing the right people to fill the positions in your cake business.

Follow these procedures when hiring employees:

- Obtain a federal employment identification number by filing IRS Form SS-4.
- Register with your state's employment department for payment of unemployment compensation taxes and file IRS Form 940-EZ to report your federal unemployment tax each year.
- Set up a payroll system for withholding taxes and making payroll tax payments to the IRS per IRS Publication 15, Circular E, Employer's Tax Guide.
- Get workers' compensation insurance and alert new hires of their rights to workers' compensation benefits.
- Familiarize yourself with Occupational Safety and Health Administration (OSHA) requirements and prepare an Injury and Illness Prevention Plan.
- Contact the federal Department of Labor and your state labor office for information on notices you must post.

- Create an employment application for each type of position.
- Create an employee handbook.

Payroll

The easiest way to make sure your payroll is handled efficiently is to outsource it. Hire a bookkeeper or accountant to help you get set up; or, purchase Quicken Home and Business (Intuit), QuickBooks (Intuit), or similar small business accounting software. You do not want to get to the end of the year and find out that you've forgotten to withhold the right amount of taxes from an employee's paycheck. If you offer benefits like health insurance and retirement, or if you have employees who receive federal earned income credit payments, this can complicate payroll even further.

The small fee charged by a local accountant or payroll firm will be well worth the cost. If you cannot afford to hire a payroll company, invest in payroll software that will calculate federal, state, and local tax withholdings. Paychex.com is a good solution for simplifying your payroll, or – if you're already using QuickBooks to manage your bookkeeping – consider Intuit Payroll. http://payroll.intuit.com/

Business Accounting Software

Business accounting software assists you with your financial recording needs, which should be meticulously recorded. If you're starting out small and are comfortable with an online solution, you can begin with the free versions of QuickBooks or Outright and work your way to the paid version as your business grows.

Once you need a pro solution, you can purchase the software and hire a bookkeeper or accountant to help you get set up and explain what you need to record. Today's accounting software keeps track of transactions that, in the past, were required to be recorded manually in a ledger. Once the business accounting software records the information, it is capable of performing functions such as running reports, analyzing expenditures, computing cost of goods sold, and more.

Typical business accounting software packages can download expenses directly from your credit card and bank accounts, so make sure you keep personal accounts and business transactions separate. QuickBooks can handle functions such as accounts payable, accounts receivable, profit and loss statements and payroll. It's like having a CPA living in your computer.

Managing Profits

In the first years of your business, your profits should be reinvested into the business as much as you can afford to do so. Do you need a company car, or do you need to advertise a specialty service you're offering?

Many business owners get caught up in the idea that they need to look like they own a business, and pull profits out of the company for frivolous things. If you want your cake business to grow and thrive, you need to reinvest in it as much as possible. Living lean in the first few years can ensure that you're around for the long haul.

Managing Vendors

Building relationships with vendors is crucial. Not only will it be difficult for you to secure credit when you first open your business because of your lack of credit rating, but it will take time to understand how much you need in supplies, meaning you may be calling your vendor to place a special order when you suddenly run short. At the same time, you should not rely solely on one vendor to provide all that you need. What if the vendor goes out of business or suddenly raises prices? Over-reliance on a single vendor can be devastating to a small business.

Effective vendor management requires you to understand what you need to run your business, know which vendors can meet your needs, and seek the most competitive prices and service levels possible. Vendor management is often overlooked as part of the business management process, but building mutually beneficial relationships with your vendors ensures that quality ingredients and supplies are available for your business when you need them.

Tips for Effective Vendor Management

Establish a liaison: Whether it is you or another employee in your business, establish clear lines of responsibility within your business for vendor management. Your vendors should have specific contacts within your business with whom they can develop a relationship. Your vendor manager should have good negotiation and organization skills, and be able to communicate your needs clearly.

Develop Strategic Partnerships: Is there a store with which you can develop a relationship that benefits you both? Looking for ways to enhance both of your businesses converts a vendor into a partner.

Clear Communication: The best success comes when you are clear about your business needs. Work out any concerns you have before entering into any kind of long-term arrangement. Be sure the vendor will be able to grow with you.

Fair, but Air-tight Contracts: The details of your relationship with your vendor should be clearly spelled out in your contract. The contract should cover all the main concerns of both parties, and should be fair to both as well.

Create a Vendor Database: Having the supplies and ingredients you need keeps your customers happy, so always have backup vendors. Create a database of available vendors with notes about what they can provide for you. The last thing you want is an interruption in your ability to meet your customers' needs because you couldn't get the ingredients needed to make all the products you normally offer.

Managing Expenses

Gross Profit Margin is the difference between the sales you generate in your business and the cost paid out to create your product. Here is a simple example: If it costs you $0.80 to make a treat and you sell it for $2.50, your gross profit is $1.70 and your gross profit margin is 68%. Keep in mind that you must calculate all of your sales and expenses related to producing your cakes when creating this ratio. Your gross profit margin is a good indication of the health of your business, revealing the proportion of money left over from revenues to pay fixed expenses and for future savings. A gross profit margin is also a concrete number you can use to establish credit, obtain loans, and grow your business. One of the best ways to improve your gross profit margin is by managing your expenses. Selling more cakes does not necessarily mean more profit if your expenses are too high. Moreover, you have much more control over how much you spend than over the customers who choose to buy from you.

By reducing your expenses, you can lower your breakeven point, which means it becomes easier to make a profit.

There are many things you can do to control expenses:

- Negotiate better prices with vendors.
- Don't make more products or store more inventory than you need.
- Make sure your prices are high enough to make a profit without chasing customers away.
- Choose a few high-profit-margin items to sell like coffee.
- Analyze your cash flow and address leaks. For example: utility bills could be lowered with motion detectors and energy-saving compact fluorescent light bulbs; or, consider eliminating expensive ingredients that don't yield a superior product.

Have you ever wondered why some bakeries or small food producers close for the day as soon as they sell out? At first glance it seems like they should stay open later and make more products, right? Obviously there is a greater demand than supply if they are selling out. However, this business practice protects the owner and their gross profit margin. Based on their food cost and analysis, they know they are profitable if they sell out. Their labor and utility costs are capped. But, if they fire up the ovens again, using additional resources and paying for additional utilities and labor, they run the risk of creating waste and lowering their profit margin. Also, it is much better for a business to track their sales over time to see if adding additional staff will increase efficiency and output that will result in higher profit, not just higher sales.

Another idea is to create a sense of demand by producing smaller quantities of lower-profit, high-demand products, and then up-selling the higher-profit comparable product. For example, a bakery will offer mini cupcakes and sell them for about a dollar less than full-size cupcakes (e.g. mini cakes sell for $1.00, full-size for $2.50). The mini cupcakes are less profitable because they are just as much labor and use almost the same amount of raw material to produce. However, consumers love them. Because they are bite-sized, customers try multiple cupcakes and they feel like they're indulging without the guilt of over-eating. The trick is to make a quantity that will sell out by the middle of the day. Customers learn to arrive early to purchase mini cupcakes, yet often purchase full-sized cupcakes to complement their order. Customers who arrive later in the day have less choice, but almost never leave empty-handed. At this point in the day, the high-profit cupcake is sold, contributing to the gross profit margin.

You've planned and planned and you're finally open for business. The hard work is done, right? What you will discover is that managing your business efficiently and profitably takes your time, determination, and energy every day. Many businesses fail because owners get through the planning stage and stop paying attention.

15
AVOIDING MISTAKES

Becoming a successful business owner takes hard work and commitment. It's easy to dream about owning your own business. The reality is that you'll end up working longer hours than when you worked for someone else, and it will be harder to leave work at the shop. Yes, you will be your own boss, and you can control the direction your company takes, but you're also at the mercy of the economy, the law, and the whims of customers.

The cake industry is physically demanding. Not only are you on your feet all day, but you're not buying five-pound bags of flour from the grocery store, but 50-pound and 100-pound bulk containers of ingredients. Heavy lifting, long hours of standing, and working late into the night to prepare for early risers is common. In addition, the work tends to be repetitious--you're often making the same things over and over again, trying to achieve a uniform look in shape, size, and design.

There are many pitfalls and challenges to face on the way to becoming a successful business owner, and there is no way to prepare for every scenario. You might be able to avoid financial or emotional distress by considering these typical mistakes and making plans now to avoid them.

Be a Business Owner, Not a Slave to Your Business

Just because you like to bake and create delicious treats, doesn't make you a good business owner. You need business sense more than you need baking sense to survive. You have to be able to wear several hats, from baker to boss, from chief bottle washer to menu planner. Make sure you don't get so wrapped up in the creative side of things that you forget to run a tight business with accurate records, paid bills, and attention to safety. Be willing to surround yourself with legal and accounting professionals who can help you understand the financial and legal aspects of the business, and remember that if you can't turn a profit by being capable of managing expenses and making smart business decisions, you will not survive. Don't be afraid to seek advice from experienced business owners, either in your retail area or through online forums.

Don't succumb to the pressure that can come with being a new business owner and giving everything away. Your friends, if they are excited about your new business, should pay for the treat or coffee when they come in; the customer should not get a free product just because you don't have the cake they prefer.

Watch Start-Up Costs

One of the ways new business owners fail is by getting spend-happy in the first few months, trying to buy everything they might possibly need. Only buy what you truly need, and be disciplined with your costs. Some of the major costs you will want to manage carefully and control, involve labor, supply, and marketing.

Develop a budget so that you can track your money and decide how much you need to make to break even and make a profit. You need to have a good understanding of your costs as well as the ability to forecast your income. Some costs to consider are:

- Cost of goods
- Salaries/wages/contract labor
- Rent/mortgage
- Utilities
- Loan payments/contract payments
- Lease payments
- Insurance premiums
- Advertising
- Transportation
- Office supplies

There is a sample budget worksheet in the resources section of our website to get you started. Adjust the worksheet to account for additional costs your business might have.

Be Flexible

To be successful, you need to be flexible. You need to be willing to work long hours, take risks, and understand that opening a business is a huge undertaking. It's easy to underestimate how much it will cost, and overestimate how quickly you will become profitable.

Plan on obtaining 40-50% more capital than you think you'll need, because you will probably need it. You will not only be contending with the development of your own business, but also with the unpredictability of the market, your competition, and the economy.

Commit for the Long-Term

Make sure you are ready to commit to the business for the long haul. It will take 12-18 months for the business to take off and for you to find your groove as a business owner. Be patient and tenacious. As a business owner, your number one goal is to establish and build your business.

Don't Try To Do It All Yourself

You may need at least one employee to answer phones and manage sales while you're doing the baking, or you won't make enough money to survive. All it takes is burning $100 in products when you're selling a $2 cake, to make you realize how incredibly important a second person can be.

Hire and Manage Employees Well

Good employees are hard to find and the cake business, like other areas of retail, has a higher level of turnover. When choosing employees, be sure you refrain from asking anything illegal (you can't ask if someone is married or planning to have kids and whether or not that would impact their availability, for example, and you can't ask about religion). A complete checklist for interviewing potential employees is in the Appendix.

As a business owner, you want to find employees who will represent your business well. This is less about whether or not they have piercings, and more about whether or not they come to work clean, dressed appropriately, and can smile readily and make your customers feel welcome. There are some aspects of customer service that simply cannot be trained. When you're getting ready to hire your staff, there are certain things you should keep in mind during the interview and due diligence process.

Past History: No matter how nice the person seems during the interview, you should call references and previous employers to verify the information provided and learn what you can about the person's previous employment. Former employers will often rave about good ex-employees and say nothing about bad ones. Listen to that silence.

Presentability: It may seem like common sense, but if your prospective employee doesn't care enough to dress professionally for the interview, how can you trust that he or she will care about the customer?

Personality: When choosing an employee, how you get along with the person and how you think that person will get along with your customers is important. Friendliness, self-confidence, enthusiasm, and honesty are critically important, particular for your front counter help.

Minimum Staff Needed

Depending on the size of your establishment and the amount of business you do, you may be able to get away with just one assistant or you may need a full staff. For the standard cake business, depending on how elaborate your treats are, the typical number of employees may include a baker, a dishwasher, a decorator, and a counter person. Don't over-hire, but don't sell the business short, either. You need people to help you run the business.

Policies and Procedures

One of the most important things you can do for your business, both while you are running it and when you're ready to exit the business, is to have well-written, clear and concise policies and procedures. Each position should have clear responsibilities and the shop as a whole should operate under a set of policies that make your expectations about harassment, food safety, and performance, crystal clear.

You should also determine what benefits you will offer and prepare a benefits manual that clearly states when an employee is eligible and what kinds of benefits are available.

Take Care of Your Equipment

Careful maintenance of your equipment, whether you are a home-based or commercial business, can save you hundreds to thousands of dollars in repair bills. These unexpected repairs can be the difference between a profitable month and an unprofitable one. Being conscientious about your gear can be as easy as regularly cleaning your equipment. Also, don't put off scheduled maintenance on critical equipment such as refrigeration, ovens, and mixing equipment. These are the lifeblood of any cake business and you can't afford to have them break down during critical times of the year.

Suggestions for maintaining your equipment:

- Clean your gear every day to prevent dirt build-up. This build-up comes from batter, frosting, and other food material falling into the crevasses. It will wear down motors, vents and fans, thereby reducing the lifespan of your equipment.
- Keep a schedule for cleaning, calibrating ovens, checking refrigerator temperatures, and de-scaling dishwashers. Hobart mixers require professional servicing to maintain the correct weight of grease and oil in very specific spots. Have it checked by an authorized provider according to the maintenance schedule.
- Closely read and follow the cleaning directions in the manual and on the solvent bottles to avoid damaging your equipment.
- Contact the manufacturer if you aren't certain of the proper way to clean any baking equipment. Most manufacturers keep copies of maintenance manuals, even for retired models, and many are online.
- Set up a service contract for your restaurant equipment with the manufacturer or a local service company to perform regularly scheduled fine-tuning of each piece.

- When choosing new equipment, opt for ones that are easy to clean. (This means coming apart and being put together easily.)
- Take advantage of your manufacturer's representatives. They are well trained and don't charge to help out, so call them to teach you the best cleaning methods for your equipment.

16
GET ORGANIZED

Lists are the key to organizing the start-up process and once you're open for business, the day-to-day work and time management.

Start-Up Processes and Planning

The following checklist provides a complete rundown of steps (many of which are detailed in previous chapters) most cake businesses must take to open their doors.

Table 7

	Administrative
	Set up as legal entity
	LLC, S-Corp, Sole Proprietor, Other
	Choose a Company Name
	Trademark Search
	Locate physical address or if home business, research regulations
	Registration of company with Secretary of State
	DBA if needed
	Credit Sheet Established, Vendor Credit Established
	If LLC: All initial, minimal legal documents
	Articles of Organization
	Pick Member or Manager Managed
	Select registrant
	Tax Setup (Partnership, S-Corp) Decision
	Apply for EIN
	Form 2553 federal tax form for S-Corp or C-Corp
	Local business license if required
	Insurance
	General Liability Policy
	Auto (if making deliveries)
	Other (Business Interruption, Property, Workers Comp Unemployment, Spoilage)

Office set up

Identify space in home

Order safe for petty cash

Organize electronic documents on GoogleDocs,Dropbox for easy sharing

Set up office equipment such as printer, fax

Set up separate phone line or Google Voice service

Create important phone numbers list

Eliminate any personal activity in business office space

Strategic Setup

Write up: Your Why

Write up: Values & Vision

Write up: Mission Statement

Write up: SWOT Analysis

Marketing Planning

Competitive Analysis

Ideal Customer Definition - Detailed Questionnaire

- Who exactly is your ideal customer?
- How do they feel when they buy your cakes, cupcakes, etc.?
- Why do they feel that way?
- How do they visualize their satisfaction?

Business Plan

Market Analysis

Financial

Pre-Startup Budget, Initial Tool, Bottoms Up

Sales Model

Cash Flow Model

Financial Projections

Create plan for raising capital

Decide on emphasis / what capital sources to focus on.

Crowdfunding options

Banking Options

Non-Banking Options

Investor Presentation

Licensing

Apply for all required licenses and permits

Complete foodhandlers training

Schedule health inspection

Branding

Brand Identity

Market positioning

Design business cards, menus, signage, uniform etc.

Schedule photoshoot for cakes/products

Marketing/PR

Website

Acquire domain

Develop Website

Choose email/shared calendar provider

Setup email addresses and client systems

Research and establish keyword list - use spyfu.com

Develop Landing Page or Launch Page

Sign up for Email mktg / mktg automation system - e.g. Mail Chimp

Set launch date for Website/Landing Page

Acquire contact info for visitors and investors ("sign up for more details...")

Create drip campaign about launch

Setup a blog site (within your website/landing page

Develop Marketing Calendar

Write initial blog posts

Publish initial blog posts

Finalize and submit hours, location, phone number, contact info, etc.

Local Marketing

Contact local press and food blogs about new business

Where/when to have a farmer's market booth/table

Network, network, network

Local Restaurants, coffee shops, small grocers - get out and meet people

Get introductions

Chamber of Commerce

Social Media Planning

What venues to focus on - Twitter, Facebook, LinkedIn, Google+

Get going on Twitter

Setup a Facebook Business page

Setup a LinkedIn page

Engage in conversation on local sites/forums

Social Media Implementation Schedule

Join LinkedIn Groups for target market

Build list of contacts

Write and post initial Blog postings

Facebook postings/Q&A initial

Operational

Financial Operations

Hire bookkeeper

Setup Quickbooks

Setup Payroll/Distribution policy

Setup initial expense policies & procedures, system (Expensify)

Setup initial payment policies & procedures

	Normalize budget with chart of accounts
	Import budget into Quickbooks
	Financial Reporting schedule
	Keep personal funds separate from business - no co-mingling
	Tax Planning
	Business Medical Insurance
	Monitor Cash Flow
	Develop/Review Contracts
	Professional Development
	Webinars/Teleseminars on Relevant Subjects (cake decorating to business)
	Paid learning programs
	Company Operations
	Design systems
	Document business systems
	Review and Update business systems
	Setup document management/version control/sharing tool
	Smallwares http://www.webstaurantstore.com
	Determine small wares requirements from equipment list
	Price and order smallwares
	Place order for paper goods (cake and cupcake boxes cupcake liners etc.)
	Product Management
	Finalize Menu
	Finalize Recipes
	Finalize Kitchen Set-up
	Calculate Food Costs
	Set up ordering system
	Identify and set up storage
	Place initial ingredient order
	Shared/rented kitchen
	Research and evaluate kitchen locations
	Complete food-handlers training
	Set up storage
	Begin receiving nonperishable items
	Home-based kitchen
	Confirm cottage food law rules and requirements
	Research and finalize kitchen equipment decisions
	Order necessary equipment and supplies
	File warranties on all equipment
	Test equipment with common recipes
	Set up storage
	Begin receiving nonperishable items

Table 7: Start-up Work Plan

As you work on your business plan and complete the steps to start your business, you should also be documenting information on paper. There is so much information that a start-up must provide to others including financial institutions, vendors, employees, etc. Here are a few documents you will likely need whether you were starting a home business or a retail operation. Prepare and keep these in a large three-ring-binder called Operations Manual. We've included our most popular checklists in the resources section of our website, so be sure to download and use them.

Operations Manual

Business Fundamentals

Important Numbers List (attorney, insurance agent, accountant, etc.)

Equipment Maintenance Records

Product Materials

Recipes

Product Guide Descriptions (Chapter 6)

Operational Forms:

Opening Procedures

Policies

Health Inspection Process

Daily health/safety checklists

Financial Records and Resources

Contract Template

Daily Sales Sheet

Vendor List

Credit Sheet

Table 8

<Your Name> Credit Sheet	
Company Name:	
Buyer:	Owner:
Phone:	Secondary Phone
Fax:	Email:

EIN#:	Reseller #:		
Bill To:			
Address:			
City:	State:		Zip:
Ship To:			
City:	State:		Zip:
Principle Bank:			
City:	State:	Zip:	Phone:
Credit References:			

Co.Name	Co.Name
Contact:	Contact:
Phone:	Phone:
Address:	Address:
Zip:	Zip:
Co.Name	Co.Name
Contact:	Contact:
Phone:	Phone:
Address:	Address:
Zip:	Zip:

Table 8: Sample Credit Sheet

Contracts Pending

Next, set up another three-ring-binder called **Contracts Pending**. This notebook will contain:

- The original and a copy of the signed agreement
- Any sketches, color samples, magazine clippings, and other design inspiration pieces
- "Important Information" list:
  - Names of everyone connected with the order: For weddings you will want to capture the bride, groom, mother of the bride, wedding planner. Be sure to make a particular note of the person who is responsible for payment.
  - Addresses, phone numbers, email addresses: Include exact address of reception site and the couple's new address after the wedding (if her address will change).

- Directions to reception site and, more importantly, specific instructions on the reception location once you arrive.
- Delivery Day Cell Phone Numbers (for emergency use only!). This list should include cell phone and all other phone numbers for the bride, mother of the bride, maid of honor, person at reception site in charge of the event, florist, photographer, and caterer.

Production Schedule

Lastly, in a third three-ring-binder, called **Production Schedule** you will create a series of checklists that will guide your daily work effort. Once you have employees you will likely return to these lists to coordinate roles and responsibilities. Making lists and writing them down is the best way to avoid mistakes and the key to getting your orders completed on time with less stress. If you are someone who is averse to making lists because you prefer the creative side of baking or because you are "not a detail person," then making lists is even more important! Lists help you track your production workflow, your financial record keeping, marketing, employee schedule, supply chain management, and much more. Equally important are the health and safety checklists that help you and your employees maintain a clean baking and serving environment, and assure successful inspections.

A cake decorator's reputation rests not only on the presentation and taste of his or her cakes, but also on the professionalism he or she exhibits upon every contact with a potential customer or colleague in the special events industry--whether by telephone, online, or face-to-face.

Take the time to list everything that must be done to fulfill each day's work and each contract frees the mind to be creative.

Production Schedule Checklists:

- "One Month Before Delivery" checklist
- "One Week Before Delivery" to-do list
- "Day Before Delivery" to-do list
- "Delivery Day" to-do list
- "Follow-Up" to-do list

The detailed nature of the sample lists below ensures that nothing is forgotten, no last-minute fires must be put out, and the cake decorator appears totally professional every step of the way, particularly on the day of delivery. This is the only way to accomplish large catered events. Note: Like all of our sample documents, these lists should be customized for your business and circumstances.

ONE MONTH BEFORE DELIVERY DATE

- If supply is low, purchase non-perishable items, such as:
    - Decorator tips
    - Clean boxes for transporting cakes
    - Cake "containers" (boxes, gift boxes, tins, cellophane bags)
- Take inventory of other items that are normally on hand, but which may be running low:
    - Pastry bags
    - Cellophane bags (if wrapping individually)
    - Packing tape
    - Paste food colors
    - Meringue powder
    - Confectioner's sugar
    - Plastic wrap
- Write a list of all grocery items to be purchased each week.
- Assemble your decorative delivery cake box or boxes. Prepare "delivery kit." A delivery kit contains:
    - Business cards
    - Copy of the signed agreement
    - Catalog or price list (for future orders, new items, specials)
- Check records to make sure balance of payment has been received or that the client's account is in good standing.

ONE WEEK BEFORE DELIVERY DATE

- Purchase all cake and icing ingredients.
- Make buttercream /royal icing and refrigerate.
- Pull all necessary pans and cooling racks.
- Clean car or van interior. Wash sheets that will be used to cover van seat and floor surfaces.
- Fill delivery vehicle with gasoline.

DAY (OR TWO) BEFORE DELIVERY

- Remove buttercream /royal icing, if applicable, from the refrigerator and allow it to come to room temperature.
- Bake and decorate cakes.
- Package cakes.
- Photograph cake, if the design is unique.
- Prepare car or van for loading tomorrow. Place magnetic business sign on vehicle.

DELIVERY DAY

- Complete any unfinished packing.
- Load delivery vehicle:
  - Delivery kit (see contents list above)
  - Cakes
  - Directions to delivery site: If you own a GPS, make sure you bring it and that the directions are loaded into it before you leave.

FOLLOW UP

- Mail thank-you notes to the party involved in the order or payment.
- If the delivery was for a party or catered event, write notes to site/event manager, caterer, and party host/hostess. The purpose of this note is to say that you enjoyed working with them and look forward to opportunities to work together in the future. Enclose your business card. Contact with these people will hopefully lead to referrals.
- Quarterly mailings to all of your customers remind them to order from you when their next "cake occasion" arises. If your customers and potential customers are reminded every three months that you decorate cakes, they are much more likely to call you. The thank-you note that you send to the client should not be the last time she hears from you.

Time Management

The most precious commodity on earth is time. We all have exactly the same amount of time each day to invest in activities that matter to each of us, or to spend doing things that are soon forgotten. The wise person invests her/his time in things that truly matter to her/him.

The time you put into your cake business is an investment because it yields a great return in your personal satisfaction and it yields a financial return.

In business, time is money! When you begin to implement time management strategies in your cake business, you will have more time to make cakes; therefore, your business will become more financially profitable. As you gain experience in making and selling cakes, you will develop your own strategies to work faster and more efficiently. The following tips are offered to assist you in reaching a level of time management in your cake business that others obtain only through trial and error--and lots of time.

Work Sooner, Not Later

As soon as an order is taken, begin a list of the steps you can do ahead of time. The goal is to keep your actual baking time to a minimum during the final days and hours before delivery or pick-up. In many cases, the final stages of design can boil down to icing or decorating the cake.

Baking Efficiency

Pre-measure: Whether you are preparing to bake a dozen cakes or five dozen, put all the ingredients on the counter before mixing the cake dough or icing. Measure all the ingredients in advance, setting aside each ingredient container after it is measured.

Multiple cakes: When baking several cakes, begin mixing dough for the second cake about 10 minutes before the first cake is completely baked. When the first cake is removed from the oven, the second cake will be ready to slide into the oven.

Record success: Keep a record of baking time for particular recipes. You will always want to test each cake to make sure it is ready, but this record will let you know when to begin checking the cake.

Eliminate uncertainty: Be sure to rewrite and test your recipes in multiples long before you need them. Attempting to double or triple a recipe under the pressure of a deadline leads to mistakes and wasted profit.

Know your mixer: Experiment to find out how large a recipe (or a multiplied recipe) your mixer can handle.

Calculate ingredient amounts: When planning a large cake order, calculate how much of each ingredient will be needed in the preparation of multiple recipes. Keep your calculations for future reference when preparing orders of the same size.

Decorating Tips

Prepare icing bags: Before beginning to coat or decorate the cake, fill all icing bags with the various colors of icing. Fill a bag with white for borders, etc. Put the appropriate tip on each bag and pull other tips that will be used with those same colors.

Consider similar colors: When using several colors to decorate one cake or an "assembly line" of several cakes, consider similar icing colors. If pale pink and a deeper rose color will be used, mix the pale pink icing; decorate with that color, then re-mix the same icing with rose coloring to deepen the already-pink color.

Borders: When decorating several cakes at once, use the same tip for each cake's borders, if possible. If not, apply all the borders that use the same tip. Change tips and complete each cake's borders.

17

DELIVERY

Whether you are a home-based bakery or operate in a commercial space, completing the transaction -- delivery of the cake to the customer -- requires just as much thought, attention to detail and professionalism as all the previous steps. You want to ensure that after all of your hard work and investment, this final effort is as seamless and simple as possible for you and your clients.

In a perfect world, plenty of time would be available between deliveries so that you are never rushed. The truth is that many bakers find themselves working right up until the last minute before delivery.

When making your lists, determine what you must do to allow yourself some down time before you leave for the clients you serve. The amount of time between the completion of baking an order(s) must include time for you to do any necessary paperwork (billing, accounting, etc.) and to clean up from your work. Whenever possible, try to allow at least an hour. This allows time for a quick shower and a quick bite to eat before rushing off to deliver your cakes.

Delivery Charges

Delivery companies are legitimate businesses that often charge hefty fees. The delivery service that you provide for your customers could almost be looked at as a separate business. Offering your cake delivery service is excellent customer service, but you should never hesitate to charge for that service. You want to promote your business as offering only the freshest ingredients, delivered in the timeliest manner. Many people will pay a premium for this.

Before determining your delivery fees, find out what other related businesses charge for delivery in your area. Also, call delivery services and ask if they will deliver your cakes and how much they would charge. You probably would never hire a 3rd-party to make your deliveries, but you may feel better about your delivery fees when you find out what they would charge!

Identify the area within which you are willing to deliver. Use a map and divide it into various delivery zones. If all things were equal, you could simply draw circles around your location on the map to determine various pricing zones. Consider traffic patterns and real drive time when dividing your map. Charge more for greater distances and/or greater potential traffic. If you are near a large metropolitan area, for example, you might charge a premium to deliver in the downtown area at 5:30 on a Friday evening.

When calculating delivery fees, consider time spent loading and unloading the cakes, actual round-trip drive time, parking fees, tolls, gas, mileage, and wear-and-tear on your vehicle. These real costs to you necessitate that you charge for delivery in order to retain the profit calculated into your product. If a client ever balks at this charge, you may offer free, scheduled pick-ups. You may consider exceptions of course, such as free delivery to your best recurring customers. A typical delivery charge in our area is about $45.00 for the first 5-10 miles with an additional charge .25 – .50 cents for each additional mile.

Web Resource: IRS.gov

For local delivery, we recommend using the IRS mileage values to set rates:

[http://tinyurl.com/cakebusiness16]

(Note, you cannot deduct mileage on your taxes for any fees which you charge the customer.)

Another variable to consider is the difficulty of reaching the delivery location. Mountain resorts for example, or rural locations, require a premium delivery fee. This is all part of the client education process and should be indicated on your website and contracts.

Delivery Process

Prior to the day of the delivery, determine when you must leave your home to arrive on time. Allow plenty of time to drive to the reception site. Drive slower than normal, and take corners carefully. Consider ordering a "Cake in Delivery" magnetic car sign so other drivers know why you're moving at a snail's pace. Vehicle magnetic signs turn your car into a business vehicle (a tax deduction) and can be ordered online from iprint [iprint.com].

If your vehicle does not have built-in GPS, consider investing in a mobile GPS device. A GPS has become a standard piece of equipment for any business offering delivery services.

Each day before a delivery, check your vehicle. If your car or van is full of fast food wrappers, library books, homework, and other odds-and-ends, remove everything that could fly into and damage your cake(s). Vacuum the interior. Pet hair, crumbs, and dirt of any kind could ruin a cake and your reputation. If you will be transporting products in the trunk, clean it thoroughly and remove all loose items. Drive through a car wash. No one wants to see any food item delivered in a dirty vehicle!

If you can drive a minivan, you will love the abundant space it provides as a cake delivery vehicle. The latest models that offer stow-and-go seats are perfect for deliveries! Other vehicles can be a little more challenging when delivering large wedding cakes or tiers. It's better to have cakes in a large, dark, flat trunk than in the cab of a car with many windows. However, tiers can be transported in trunks, on car floors, and on seats. Measure all of these areas in your vehicle and do the math to determine where and how each tier will be loaded. If some boxes will be placed on seats and seats are not level, try placing folded towels on the seat to make the surface more level. Use a nonskid rubber mat or egg-crate foam pad to protect cakes. In lieu of rubber mats, use slightly damp (not wet) cloths under cake boxes to avoid sliding.

Use baker's boxes whenever possible. For assembled cakes, label each section clearly so you are not searching during assembly, and use a checklist to make sure you have the entire cake. If some tiers are too large or stacked too high, use clean cardboard boxes. Whenever possible, wait until you arrive at the reception site to stack your tiers.

Transportation of your cakes should also be considered through the lens of food safety. Be mindful of the temperature of the vehicle's interior. Turn on air conditioning in your vehicle before loading the cake(s) and load everything else before finally loading the cake. Use plenty of cool packs in addition to the air conditioning. These simple steps will help prevent icing from melting. Fondant has the tendency to weep if exposed to quickly changing hot and cool environments, so try to move from cool space to cool space quickly. If possible, keep the cake away from or cover the windows, and use insulated boxes if available. A large insulated box or cover can be made by duct-taping or gluing together sheets of foil-backed insulation foam from the hardware store.

Be sure stacked cakes have a long, sharpened dowel through the center of tiers. This is not a step to skip.

Web Resource:Wilton.com

http://bit.ly/MNjBA7

Wilton offers even more great advice on transporting and delivering your cakes.

Wedding Cake Deliveries

Prior to arrival, contact a person at the hotel or hall to confirm your delivery and verify that the cake table will be ready. Ask the contact person if there is a loading dock or service elevator, or ask for the best entrance to use. Are there several different banquet rooms at this location? If so, which room will you be delivering to? Will the air conditioning be on?

The first rule to remember when arriving at the reception site is always to leave your car locked when you step away from it. On hot days, leave the car air conditioning on while taking each tier inside. Always keep an extra set of keys in your pocket. Upon entering the building, find the person in charge of this event, introduce yourself and offer your business card. This person's name should appear on the signed agreement. They should be expecting you as you just called them to confirm everything was ready. Scout out the site before you carry anything in. Ask the "person in charge" to show you the cake table and confirm that the table is in the proper place and will not be moved. Check the table for levelness and stability. Also, confirm that the drapes or coverings on the tables are all in place.

Ask for the location of the exterior entry door closest to the cake table and make sure this door is unlocked. If you have previously requested the loan of a rolling cart, ask the manager about the cart at this time. Having your own collapsible delivery cart can come in handy, especially when you have a very heavy cake or a long way to walk. Consider investing in one.

Secure your vehicle at the curb next to the closest entry door. If possible, prop open the door and make sure the path from this door to the cake table is clear of any obstructions. Bring in your delivery kit and place it on the floor beside the cake table. Do not put any of your things on any tables other than the cake table. Place a sign on the table that reads: "Cake Delivery in Process, Please Do Not Disturb" and your cell phone number.

Next, bring in the cake. If you car is blocking a delivery area, place another "Cake Delivery in Process," sign in the dash. Move your car as soon as the cake is inside.

After the cake is completely set up, carefully remove everything from the cake table and clean up everything in the area where you worked. Look carefully at the cake table from all angles to ensure that the cake is perfectly level and centered. Take this opportunity to photograph the cake from multiple angles.

Ask the event manager to come to the cake table and look at the cake. Ask her to sign the bottom of the agreement where it states that the cake was set up as stated in the agreement. Give her the slicing instruction sheet and the box for the top tier-the anniversary tier (if applicable). Although it is stated on the slicing instruction sheet, be sure that she understands which items are to be returned to you and point out any decorative items on that cake that are not edible.

Some bakeries charge a flat equipment deposit. You may also want to charge the replacement value (ask for a separate check, deposit, or keep the credit card on file) and tell the client that you will return the deposit when/if the items are returned. This should all be documented on the cake agreement/contract, including the time frame and condition (they should be clean) for your items' return, as well as the specific fees. If equipment is returned with missing pieces, or very late, make it clear that the renting party is responsible for additional charges. You can put your name and phone number on your plates, to assure their return. Leave a bag or box at the reception, along with a list of items to be returned to you.

Your photos of the cake immediately after set-up also serve as "proof" as to the condition of the cake when delivered. While it is rare, there are occasions when a cake decorator has had the unfortunate experience of damage done to their cakes due to circumstances beyond their control. After you leave, the caterers may try to move the table or bump into the table by accident. Children may arrive in the reception site before the wedding party and stick their fingers in the cake. Your photos-taken from all angles show that you set up the cake properly, in the agreed-upon location, and that the cake was in perfect condition when you left.

Delivery Kit

A delivery kit contains:

- Map to reception/party site
- Telephone number of site
- Telephone number of contact person
- Contract / invoice / delivery form
- Bride's top ornament
- Cutting knife and server set (in case one is not provided)
- Angled spatula
- Piping bag(s) filled with icing (one bag with each color; secure end with twist-tie and wrap in plastic wrap)
- Container of icing
- One of each decorating tips used on cake (for touch-ups, if necessary)
- Decorating bags
- Tips used to decorate the cake
- Couplers
- Spatulas
- Flowers: Fresh or silk flowers/greenery
- Flower spikes
- Picture of the cake
- Columns/pillars, plus extras (in case of necessary last-minute design changes)
- Pillar pruning shears
- Any decorations or cake topper that will be added on site
- Ribbon
- Tulle
- Tablecloths if necessary to cover ugly tables
- Florist's wire
- Scissors that can also cut wire
- Toothpicks
- Meat or kabob skewers
- Paper towels
- Wax or parchment paper
- Wet washcloth in plastic bag or moist wipes
- Dry cloth
- A level
- Shims to correct uneven tables
- Measuring tape
- Camera, extra memory card, and extra battery

- Business cards and a holder
- A congratulations card for the couple
- An ink pen
- Clear tape and double-sided tape
- Small hot-glue gun
- Dressmakers pins (for securing fabric when necessary)
- Band-aids
- Apron
- Garbage bag
- Latex gloves
- Doorstop
- Extension cords
- Duct tape
- Distilled water
- Color for water
- Flower holder ring

For the Bride

- Cutting/serving instructions specific to this cake
- Latex gloves for the server(s)
- Box for anniversary cake
- List of pieces to be returned
- Box or bag for plates and columns

Business Delivery

As with weddings, delivery to your wholesale clients is a critical part of customer service and will help determine future opportunities. In addition to the guidelines for wedding deliveries, the following are a few ideas to keep in mind:

Smile: One of the most important things you can do when completing any transaction, be it in your home, your shop, or at a customer's place of business, is to smile. The people with whom you are interacting may be stressed out or hurried, but part of a great customer service experience is the positive communication you provide.

Look Sharp: It is important to arrive at the delivery site looking neat and professional. There is no need to "dress up"--keep it casual, but neat. A "uniform" for deliveries might be freshly pressed khaki pants or shorts and a clean, white T-shirt topped by an oxford cloth (dress) shirt, tucked in with sleeves rolled up. The restaurant manager or shopkeeper will be on hand when you arrive. Each of these people will take note of your professionalism.

Get to Know Your Client: Take every opportunity to develop a relationship with your customers. If you are working with a larger store or venue, get to know the person in charge of accepting deliveries. Often the shops that deal with specialty food items are small family-run businesses, so it will be easy to recognize many of the employees. Take the time to introduce yourself. Learn their names, and when appropriate, engage in conversation. While you should keep this kind of chatting brief, making connections is part of the business and can help encourage long-term relationships.

Get it On Paper: When dropping off an order, request that the responsible party sign a receipt for the delivery once they have reviewed the order. They will sign the bottom of the agreement stating that the delivery included all of the ordered products. If for some reason you did not complete the order, or if you made an error in delivery, mark those omissions on the agreement and initial. This should be noted in the billing.

Hiring Delivery Help

When your business grows and your delivery schedule becomes overwhelming, you may consider hiring someone to deliver your cakes or asking a family member to help. Before hiring someone to make a solo delivery, ask the person you are considering for the job to assist you in several deliveries. Your helper (and you) must be totally confident in their ability to deliver safely and on-time. This person must also be able to collect payments, take additional orders, or promote your business, so don't rush into a decision without first seeing them interact with others.

Whomever you hire (even a family member) must be as professional in every way as you are in your dealings with clients. When you reach the point of needing delivery assistance, you have already developed a stellar reputation. Protect your reputation by hiring only the best. If you use a third party delivery service, make sure they have experience in cake delivery, will represent you well, and have a refrigerated vehicle.

Shipping

The shipping of specialty foods, including baked goods is much more common thanks to ecommerce, improved packaging processes and technologies, and customer demand. Online ordering is a familiar way to shop for many people, particularly for products where customization is not essential such as cupcakes, cake pops, non-decorated cakes, etc. If you plan to offer online ordering, shipping is an issue you will have to address. First, selling and shipping food across state lines is under the jurisdiction of the FDA. While many small home bakers sell food on sites like Etsy, they may not be taking the regulations into account and could be in violation of the law. If you wish to sell and ship nationally, contact the FDA (FDA.gov) to determine the requirements for doing so.

Cakes, including bar cakes such as brownies, cupcakes, and cake pops are durable foods that ship well, as long as they are shipped correctly. The most important thing to remember is that the outside of any package should clearly be marked "PERISHABLE." Usually, the best way to ship is overnight in a Styrofoam container, frozen and packed with dry ice. Using this method, the package may sit for up to 12 hours after delivery before proper storage is required.

If you're not sure how well a food item will ship, test it. Place the food in a container and shake it a few times. If it holds its shape, it should ship well. To see if the food retains moisture well, place the food in a draft (made by a fan or wind). We often order baked goods from different bakeries to discover new methods, best practices and pricing.

Materials: Start by putting in a layer of packing material in a sturdy corrugated box. Next, center the package in the middle of the styrofoam container and place that container inside the outer box. Then, overfill the box with cushioning material, making sure there's no air space left in the box.

Boxes: You should have three basic lines of defense: an inner "gift" box that is well-packed in an insulated/styrofoam box, inside a third, outer heavy corrugated box, suitable for shipping. When choosing an outer box, make sure it's roomy enough to allow plenty of packing material on all sides. Check with your carrier on the sizes that can be sent.

Using Tins: When sending cakes in a tin, place a piece of bubble wrap on the bottom of the container, then line the container with parchment paper or cellophane, leaving enough to tuck over the top once the container is fully packed. Place one layer of cakes in the container. Cover with parchment paper. Arrange another layer of cakes, followed with more parchment paper, and continue this layering until the container is full. Tuck the cellophane or parchment paper over the top, then place another piece of bubble wrap on top, and seal your container.

Pack the tin in a box, neatly lined with lengths of bubble wrap, and then fold the bubble wrap back into the margins between the tin and the box to form a double cushion. Toss a scoop or two of packing popcorn at the bottom of the box. Set the cake tin on top, and surround it with more packing popcorn.

Choose a box that is appropriate in size to the cake tin(s) within. This will help keep the tins from shifting and the cakes from breaking. The ideal cushion is two to three inches of packing material on all sides.

Cushioning materials: These can include recycled Styrofoam, bubble wrap, and Eco Foam, the environment-friendly cousin of foam peanuts or other packing materials that are safe to use with food. Eco Foam is a biodegradable cornstarch product that provides excellent cushioning; however, there are potential problems. Its main drawback is that it melts when wet, so don't use it to pack any containers that may leak. With popcorn, there have been warnings not to use any type of food as packing material when shipping, because it can attract insects. It also can absorb exhaust fumes from cargo holds and other areas the package may pass through in transit.

Styrofoam, dry ice packs: Needed when shipping perishable items. Dry ice packs should be placed inside of the Styrofoam box. Perishable items should be shipped overnight in the summer months. Second-day air is acceptable for cooler climates. Check with your carrier on the best practices and zones for shipping.

Moisture absorbers: If you are worried about moisture, there are moisture absorbers available; but be careful that you use those approved for foods, and ask whether or not the baked product will get too dry if you use them.

Packing tape and address label: Use a tape that is strong enough to withstand shipping. A clearly written shipping label is very important.

Select mode of shipping: There are many shipping providers. Each has a variety of services available. You can review what is offered, calculate shipping costs, find the nearest location, or locate the customer service telephone number on the Internet. Fed Ex and UPS have both developed entire divisions dedicated to helping small businesses ship specialty items, and are continually improving the tools to help get our products into the hands of our customers.

Web Resource: Uline.com

http://www.uline.com/

Uline is a well-known supplier of boxes, packing tape, cello bags, bakery boxes and bags, crinkle paper, stickers and shipping tags.

Due to the economies of scale, you are likely to save money over a local supplier.

18
GROWING YOUR BUSINESS

You should be continually striving for excellence in everything you do. As you get through those first difficult months and begin to catch your stride, think ahead to what you envision your business being in a year, five years, even ten years. You may be happy being a small cake business serving a community of loyal customers; but you may want growth that encompasses developing an online cake business, a franchised operation, or multiple outlets. Whatever your direction, most business owners want to grow their business and keep it thriving. There are things you can do as a business owner to help ensure the ongoing success of your business.

Ultimately, even if you decide to get out of the cake business down the road, continue growing your business so that it is easier to sell when you are ready to exit or retire. There are many things that business books or classes can't quantify, yet are so important in creating an aura to your business--that special something that helps grow a passionate, loyal following. Here are two that I think are paramount to success:

Reputation: It's very easy to tarnish a good reputation, but almost impossible to repair a bad one. The old adage that an unhappy customer tells ten people and a happy customer tells one is close to the truth. Strive to make the experience your customers have with your business the best it can be. This means addressing everything from cleanliness, food quality, the service your customers receive from you, your employees, your website, your phone presence, everything!

Word-of-mouth advertising is still the most powerful advertising you can get…especially since word of mouth typically means a post on Facebook or a review on a website that hundreds or more people may read. Make customer service training a part of every new hire's training, and think of your role as host or hostess to be as important as every other role you play as a small business owner.

Giving Back To Your Community: One of the best ways you can become a true member of your community is to become involved. Sponsor teams spend some good will money for local sports and performance program advertising, and/or are a member of your Chamber of Commerce. Host a Sweet Treats event for Valentine's Day, a Cake Decorating

Contest at Christmas, or some other community event where people can get to know your company.

If you have a shop, show pride in your community by maintaining the exterior of your business and being the type of location that enhances the area. Make people feel welcome when they visit from out of town. I know from the many cake bakeries I've visited and helped get started, that affordable locations are often not in the most elegant parts of town. While some cake shops are started in trendy urban and suburban locales, many start-ups have more humble beginnings in 'second-rate' strip malls or previously abandoned bakeries in struggling neighborhoods. The beauty for the scrappy entrepreneur is that often in these 'less desirable' venues, there is a community of start-ups, trying to reinvigorate the entire neighborhood. The run-down shop you invest in today could be in the middle of the hippest block in the city if enough momentum is there. That is why I urge new cake shops to show their community pride, no matter where they are.

Top 5 Ways to Grow Your Business

Being successful in business is hard work, but there are things you can do that will make growing your business a little bit easier.

1. Market Penetration

When most people think about business growth, they think about ways to attract new customers and extend their reach to new markets, but the first thing you should consider is how to get more and do more for your existing customer base. This is called market penetration, and it is much easier to accomplish than actually expanding your market, because you already have these customers in front of you, ready to tell you what they need.

Elicit feedback from your customers about what they wish you offered, but don't. Make sure your existing customers know about all the different services you offer. Just because Mrs. Smith only stops in to get a cake once every few months doesn't mean she wouldn't turn to you for her office's monthly coffee and desert catering needs, so make sure your customers know everything you are capable of doing. Other ways to increase your penetration:

Upsell and cross-sell complementary products to your customers: As in the example above, make sure Mrs. Smith knows about your specialty items and delivery options.

Reward regular customers: Offer punch cards or discount coupons to customers who make a purchase. Offer a free cup of coffee with every dozen cupcakes purchased, or send the customer home with 10% off the next purchase every time they buy.

2. Referrals and Word-of-Mouth

Enough emphasis cannot be placed on how important customer service is, but the best way to grow your business is to make your existing customers happy so that they will go out and talk to other people about how great you are. People are more likely to buy when someone they know says it's worth it.

- If you do any specialty services like catering or occasion-specific cakes, ask your satisfied customers and clients to refer you to others who might need your services. Offer them a discount for bringing in a referral card or mentioning the person who referred them. Entice new customers by getting your existing customers in on your marketing. For birthday cakes, this is so easy.
- Get together with other local, non-competing businesses, and put together a welcome package full of coupons that realtors can give new homeowners.

3. Extend Your Reach

Do you have the ability to deliver locally? Would your cakes be welcome at a local restaurant or shop?

There are many ways you can work to extend the reach of your business. If you build from what you already do well, it can be an easy process to adapt it to a new environment. Online shops are viable, thanks to super-fast shipping capabilities and refrigerated shipping materials. You can ship your cakes just about anywhere. (Although, check with the FDA for intrastate and international restrictions on food shipments).

- Add a shopping cart function to your website that allows people (locally and not) to place orders with you. Be sure to calculate shipping accurately and make sure you only offer items that can truly survive the shipping and transit time.
- Adding a delivery service is another great way to extend your reach, but be sure to adjust your prices overall or add a delivery fee to the total, (See Ch. 17) because no matter where you live, gas is an expensive addition to your cash outflow. Make sure, through market research, that there would be enough interest in offering delivery before actually doing it.
- Partner with a local gift shop or restaurant to display your cakes at their counter. Not only will they purchase the products from you, but you can often negotiate advertising as part of the deal, with your cake business name appearing with the item.

4. Trade Shows and Industry Networking

Attending trade shows is one of the best ways to keep up on the latest trends in the industry, make contacts with important vendors, showcase your products, and gain new clients. You do not want to spend all of your time at trade shows and neglect your business, but attending a show or two each year is smart business. Choose the shows you attend wisely, and make sure they are the best ones for your particular niche and scale of operation.

5. Differentiate Your Offerings

Draw new clientele by catering to specific niches like vegan or locally sourced ingredients. Baking trends are always emerging and changing, but it's a safe bet that small tasty indulgences will continue to be popular among a wide audience. Most importantly, do what you love to do!

Stay Focused

People who start their own businesses are often "idea people"--they are creative in their thinking and do not shy away from something new or risky. They get a kernel of an idea and are ready to run with it! They see the "big picture" immediately and, in the next instant, think of several other ideas that build upon the first. An original idea of starting a cake business idea could turn into thoughts of a full-scale bakery or even a catering business. When your friends hear of your idea to become a home-based cake business, they may ask, "Are you going to open a storefront?" or, "Are you going to offer other baked goods?"

Be prepared for your mind to start spinning with ideas of things you could do other than cakes. And, be prepared for well-meaning friends with lots of great ideas, but often no clue of what it takes to implement what they are suggesting.

If running a cake business is the business about which you are passionate, take a moment to determine your true reasons for choosing this work before adding other services or products to your business. Consider the amount of time another product or service would require. Consider additional licensing and other requirements for an add-on to your business. Consider your skill, talent, and passion for another area of business. Consider expenses and profitability. Consider the time required to build your cake business, and add to it the time necessary to add another product or service.

19
CONCLUSION

Starting any new business can be very exciting and a little frightening! When you have determined that a cake business is the way you are going to invest your time, your money, and your energy--do everything within your power to make it happen. Read everything you can find on baking, recipes, and starting a business. Talk to other bakers, wedding service providers, and owners of home-based businesses of any type.

Set goals for your business. Constantly review your goals to make sure you remain on course. When you find that something is not working for your business, find a new way to meet your needs. Take the time to complete each of the writing sections including your WHY statement and the Business Plan. Use the checklists to help you get started.

Jump start your business by committing to the goals listed below:

- Order business cards immediately.
- Test at least four cake and icing recipes within one week from today (give extra cakes to neighbors' kids).
- Hand out at least five business cards every day.
- Begin a recipe notebook this week and have at least twenty new recipes in it within two weeks.
- Practice at least three new decorated cake designs every week.
- Set up your Facebook page today and start having conversations with others online.
- Keep setting and meeting goals! As your business grows and your skill increases, set new goals. Keep challenging yourself and making yourself and your business better and better.

BEST WISHES!

Connect with me online!

My Blog: Cake-business.com

Twitter: @cakebusiness

APPENDIX

Culinary Schools with a Baking Emphasis

American Institute of Baking (AIB)

AIB is a not-for-profit corporation, founded by the North American wholesale and retail baking industries in 1919 as a technology transfer center for food processors and bakers.

Ballymaloe Cookery School, Ireland

Founded in 1983, Ballymaloe is one of Europe's foremost cookery schools. Unlike any other cookery school in the world, the school is located in the middle of a 100-acre, organic farm of which ten acres are devoted to organic market gardens, orchards, and greenhouses.

The Culinary Institute of America (CIA)

The CIA offers associate and bachelor's degree programs in Culinary Arts and Baking and Pastry Arts. Also, Continuing Education for foodservice professionals is offered both in Hyde Park, NY and St. Helena, CA.

The French Culinary Institute

The French Culinary Institute offers day and evening programs in Classic Culinary Arts, Classic Pastry Arts, as well as short Courses for the Serious Amateur and Short Pastry Courses.

Johnson and Wales University

The College of Culinary Arts offers a variety of programs for students, professionals, and food enthusiasts. Degree programs are offered in both the day school and in Continuing Education in the evenings and on weekends. The main campus is located in Providence, RI. Other campuses include Charlotte, NC; North Miami, FL; and Denver, CO

International School of Baking

Based upon the premise that fewer is better, the International School of Baking, located in Bend, Oregon, teaches rigorous classes to one or two students who work in a hands-on environment with the instructor.

Kendall College

Founded in 1984, The School of Culinary Arts and Hotel Restaurant Management at Kendall College is considered one of the leading culinary schools in the country. Students complete an intensive, sequentially organized curriculum under the direction of certified chef-instructors.

Texas Culinary Academy

Le Cordon Bleu's world-renowned culinary training in Austin, Texas, offers AAS Degrees in Culinary Arts and Hospitality, Restaurant Management, and a certificate in Patisserie and Baking.

San Francisco Baking Institute

Classes and seminars provide a strong foundation of Artisan Baking skills, an overall appreciation of baking and pastry arts, and the opportunity to flourish creatively in small, hands-on classes. Programs benefit professional bakers wishing to refine skills and techniques, bakery owners who recognize the importance of well-trained staff, and baking enthusiasts looking to change careers and open a bakery, or just have fun with serious home baking.

Professional Organizations

These organizations will be very valuable in terms of your business plan industry research. While you may not refer to these organizations very often, they can provide an invaluable service as a professional knowledge center.

American Society of Baking asbe.org/

The American Society of Baking, formerly known as the American Society of Bakery Engineers, is a professional society comprised of members who are engaged in, involved with, or interested in wholesale or large-scale bakery production.

AIB International aibonline.org

AIB International's mission is to "put science to work for the baker" AIB's staff includes experts in the fields of baking production; research related to experimental baking, cereal science, and nutrition; food safety and hygiene; occupational safety; and maintenance engineering.

American Culinary Federation (ACF) www.acfchefs.org

The American Culinary Federation, Inc. is a professional, not-for-profit organization for chefs. The principal goal of the founding chefs remains true today - to promote a professional image of the American chef worldwide through education among culinarians at all levels.

Retailer's Bakery Association (RBA) rbanet.com

Retailer's Bakery Association is a trade association creating industry-specific training programs, developing profit tools, and connecting retailers with suppliers and industry experts.

Trade Publications

Baking Business bakingbusiness.com

Publishers of three industry publications covering aspects of the baking industry, *Baking Buyer, Milling* and *Baking News*, and *Baking and Snack.*

Baking Buyer

They specialize in reporting on industry news, new product trends, and merchandising ideas for executives and entrepreneurs managing retail, in-store, food service, and niche wholesale bakeries. Each issue features the industry's leading operations, highlights, innovative marketing and product ideas, and showcases the latest equipment, ingredients, supplies, and services.

BakeryNet bakery-net.com/

BakeryNet is a storehouse of bakery information for the bakery industry professional, from the publishers of *Modern Baking* and *Baking Management.*

Modern Baking modern-baking.com/

Modern Baking is the retail bakery foods industry's most-read journal.

Baking Management baking-management.com/

Baking Management brings volume bakery managers the information they need to stay in front. While geared toward large operations, small businesses can still take advantage of the consumer research and trends.

Online Community Resources

Bake Space bakespace.com/forums/index.php

Bakery-Net bakery-net.com

Everything for the baker: buyer's guide, company listing, associations, industry news, want-ads, schools, etc.

Bakery-Net Forums forums.bakery-net.com/index.php

Chef Talk Baking Forum tinyurl.com/cupcake6

King Arthur Flour's Online Baking Classes tinyurl.com/cupcake8

Top Tastes Forum Desserts and Baking: tinyurl.com/cupcake9

Suppliers

Bakery Crafts bakerycrafts.com

Request a catalog from this very large supplier. Items include cupcake toppers, pastry bags, pastry tips, bakery labels, cupcake wrappers, bulk sprinkles, bulk edible glitter, professional equipment, cake toppers, wedding toppers, and décor.

BRP Boxshop brpboxshop.com

One of the best bakery box suppliers out there. US shipping is free and quick. Bulk cake boards. Bakery boxes for: cakes, cupcakes, pie, cookies – custom sizes and colors available.

CK Products ckproducts.com/

Everything related to cake decorating including cupcake liners, food coloring, flavoring, cutters, melting chocolates, cake pans, edible glitter, sprinkles, cupcake toppers, and more.

Decopac decopac.com/

This is the popular supplier of commercial cartoon character cake toppers. They also have candles, edibles, and sprinkles in bulk, as well as professional equipment including airbrush, pastry tips and bags, wedding items.

Hubert hubert.com
Commercial kitchen supplies and equipment. Large supplier, mostly for commercial kitchens.

Kerekes bakedeco.com
One-Stop Shop for the commercial kitchen and bakery with a diverse selection of cake decorating items.

Nashville Wraps nashvillewraps.com

Eco-Friendly food packaging including bakery boxes, ribbon, tissue paper, paper shred, tulle, cello paper, and more.

Pfeil & Holing, Inc. cakedeco.com

Supplier for professional cake decorators and businesses: Novelty cake decorations, seasonal cake decorations, royal icing decorations, molded sugar decorations, wedding cake top ornaments, pastry bags, gumpaste flowers, bakery supplies, pans, and utensils.

Rich LTD richltd.com/Retail display shelves and containers.

Internet: Flour and Ingredients

Cook Natural Products cooknaturally.com

General Mills generalmills.com

King Arthur Flour kingarthurflour.com

Lake County Walnuts lcwalnut.com

Lesaffre lesaffre.fr

Plugrá Butter plugra.com

Business Resources

International Dairy-Deli-Bakery Association iddba.org

Information on IDDBA membership, products and services, podcasts, annual expo and seminar, links to other food sites.

American Bakers Association americanbakers.org

This organization deals with legislative issues concerning the bakery industry.

Small Business Administration sba.gov

Online resource for small business information and publications

State Government Offices : Rules and Regulations

If you are considering a home-based cake business, you may be able to operate under a cottage food law. Contact your local or state-wide ***Department of Health*** *or* ***Department of Agriculture*** *for the rules that govern your community.*

Alabama alabama.gov

Department of Public Health 334-206-5375 adph.org/ENVIRONMENTAL

All permitting and inspections handled at county level.

Business License: at county level, list: ador.state.al.us/licenses/index.html

Business Structure Filing: sos.state.al.us/BusinessServices/Default.aspx

Business Name Registration/Secretary of State: sos.state.al.us/BusinessServices/Default.aspx

Department of Revenue: ador.state.al.us/bus.html

Information on Starting a Business: alabama.gov/portal/secondary.jsp?page=Business

Small Business Administration Office: sba.gov/localresources/district/al/index.html

Alaska alaska.gov

Alaska Department of Environmental Conservation, Division of Environmental Health, Food Safety and Sanitation Program;

Submit plan for approval: dec.state.ak.us/eh/fss/Food/Opening.html

State will then inspect and issue permit if everything is approved.

Business License: commerce.state.ak.us/CBP/

Business Structure Filing: commerce.state.ak.us/occ/cforms.htm

Business Name Registration: commerce.state.ak.us/occ/register.html

Business Tax Registration: tax.alaska.gov

Resources for Starting a Business alaska.gov/businessHome.html

Small Business Administration Office: sba.gov/localresources/district/ak/index.html

Arizona az.gov

Food Safety and Environmental Services azdhs.gov/phs/oeh/fses/

Health inspections handled at county level.

Business Structure Filing: azcc.gov/divisions/corporations/filings/forms/index.htm

Business Tax Registration: aztaxes.gov

Information on Starting a Business: azcommerce.com/BusAsst/SmallBiz/

Small Business Administration Office: sba.gov/localresources/district/ar/index.html

Arizona has a Cottage Food Law. All rules and regulations are posted on azdhs.gov/phs/oeh/fses/goods/index.htm.

Arkansas portal.arkansas.gov

County and City Government permits and Licensing by County

Rules and Regulations healthy.arkansas.gov/programsServices/environmentalHealth/foodProtection/Pages/default.aspx

Inspection of all food service, food processing and food storage facilities; review of all plans for food service establishments, food store and markets and other food related establishments; issuance of annual food permits; collection of samples of food products to ensure bacteriological standards are met; work with area staff to implement special projects as needed to assure program effectiveness; quality assurance through periodic evaluations of area and county programs; and technical training to professional staff and industry.

Business Structure Filing: sos.arkansas.gov/corp_ucc_business.html

Business Name Registration:sos.arkansas.gov/corp_ucc_business.html

Business Tax Registration: dfa.arkansas.gov/offices/incomeTax/Pages/default.aspx

Arkansas Small Business Development Center asbdc.ualr.edu/

Small Business Administration Office: sba.gov/localresources/district/ar/index.html

Arkansas has a Cottage Food Law exempting homemade products from Health Department oversight and allowing its citizens to operate a home-based bakery business. For details, contact the Arkansas Department of Health & Agriculture.

healthy.arkansas.gov/

aad.arkansas.gov

California ca.gov

Processed food registration 916-558-1784 Must contact local health department for licensing and inspection. Business license is handled locally.

Business Structure Filing: sos.ca.gov/business/be/forms.htm

Business Name Registration: Contact your County Recorder Clerk's Office

Business Tax Registration: taxes.ca.gov

Information on Starting a Business: in California calbusiness.ca.gov

Small Business Administration Office: sba.gov/localresources/district/ca/

Colorado colorado.gov

State Public Health Dept. 303-692-3644 cdphe.state.co.us/regulations/consumer/

All permitting and inspections handled through county.

Must obtain Sales tax license from the state.

Business Structure Filing: sos.state.co.us/pubs/business/main.htm

Business Name Registration: sos.state.co.us/biz/FileDoc.do

Business Tax Registration: colorado.gov/revenue/tax

City or County Business Licenses: Contact your local tax department

Information on Starting a Business: colorado.gov

Small BusinessAdministration Office sba.gov/localresources/district/co/index.html

Connecticut ct.gov

Dept. of Consumer Protection, 860-713-6160. Subject to state and local zoning and health laws. State requires plan review and license application followed by state inspection.

ct.gov/dcp/site/default.asp

Business license is registered with your town clerk.

Business Name Registration: ct.gov/sots/site/default.asp

Business Tax Registration: tinyurl.com/3mwj6yo

Information on Starting a Business: tinyurl.com/3jnyzzp

Small Business Administration Office: sba.gov/localresources/district/ct/index.html

DC dc.gov

Health Code Requirements and Permit dchealth.dc.gov

Office of Consumer and Regulatory Affairs, 202-442-4576

Business Structure Filing: dcra.dc.gov/DC/DCRA/

Business Name Registration: dcra.dc.gov/DC/DCRA/

Business Tax Registration: taxpayerservicecenter.com/fr500/

Information on Starting a Business: brc.dc.gov

Small Business Administration Office: sba.gov/localresources/district/dc/index.html

Delaware delaware.gov

All inspections handled at county level Department of Agriculture dda.delaware.gov/

Business Structure Filing: corp.delaware.gov/howtoform.shtml

Business Name Registration: sos.delaware.gov/

Business Tax Registration: onestop.delaware.gov/osbrlpublic/Home.jsp

Information on Starting a Business: dedo.delaware.gov

Small Business Administration Office: sba.gov/localresources/district/de/index.html

Florida myflorida.com

Health Code Requirements, Permits and inspections handled at the city and county level.

Business Licenses, Permits and Regulation myflorida.com/taxonomy/business/

Business Structure Filing: sunbiz.org

Business Name Registration: efile.sunbiz.org/ficregintro.html

Business Tax Registration: dor.myflorida.com/dor/taxes/registration.html

Information on Starting a Business: myflorida.com/taxonomy/business/

Small Business Administration Office: sba.gov/localresources/district/fl/

Florida has a Cottage Food Law allowing home-based bakeries or food processing businesses. freshfromflorida.com/fs/

Georgia georgia.gov

Environmental Health Food Service health.state.ga.us/programs/envservices/foodservice.asp

Applications and permits are issued through county but inspections by state. Contact your county health department for details.

Business Structure Filing: sos.georgia.gov/corporations/

Business Name Registration: sos.ga.gov/firststop/faqs.htm

Business Tax Registration: etax.dor.ga.gov/ctr/formsreg.aspx

Information on Starting a Business: tinyurl.com/3wjxz4v

Small Business Administration Office: sba.gov/localresources/district/ga/index.html

The State of Georgia has a cottage food law that allows "low risk" foods to be prepared at home for sale at non-profit or government sponsored Farmers' Markets within the state of Georgia. tinyurl.com/3r564vv.

For additional details about small/home food processing contact your local health department or the Georgia Department of Agriculture. agr.georgia.gov/

Hawaii hawaii.gov

Food businesses must submit plan for review and apply for permit. Contact your local health department office.

Business Structure Filing: ehawaii.gov

Business Name Registration: hbe.ehawaii.gov/BizEx/home.eb

Business Tax Registration: hbe.ehawaii.gov/BizEx/home.eb

Information on Starting a new Business hawaii.gov/dbedt/business/start_grow/

Small Business Administration Office: sba.gov/localresources/district/hi/index.html

Idaho idaho.gov

Health Code inspections handled at the city and county level.

Environmental Health, 208-327-7499

Licence application: cdhd.idaho.gov/pdfs/food/food_estab_license_app.pdf

Facility requirements: tinyurl.com/idahobakery

Business Structure Filing: sos.idaho.gov/corp/corindex.htm

Business Name Registration: sos.idaho.gov/corp/ABNform.htm

Business Tax Registration: labor.idaho.gov/applications/ibrs/ibr.aspx

Information on Starting a new Business business.idaho.gov

Small Business Administration Office: sba.gov/localresources/district/id/index.html

Illinois illinois.gov

The state has no licensing requirement at this time, though you are subject to inspection. Food Service Sanitation Code tinyurl.com/r43lhh

Health inspections are handled at the city or county health department. You must report activity to Food Processing Coordinator 217-785-2439.

Illinois County Health Departments

Adams County (IL) Health Department co.adams.il.us/health/

Bond County (IL) Health Department gvc.net/~bchd30/

Boone County Department of Public Health boonehealth.org/

Champaign-Urbana Public Health District cuphd.org/

Chicago Department of Public Health tinyurl.com/3q9qh6g

Clark County (IL) Health Department clarkcountyhealthdept.org/

Clay County (IL) Health Department healthdept.org/

Clinton County (IL) Health Department clintonco.org/health_dept.htm

Cook County Public Health Department co.cook.il.us/agencyDetail.php?pAgencyID=35

DeKalb County (IL) Health Department dekalbcountyhealthdepartment.org/

DuPage County (IL) Health Department dupagehealth.org/

Effingham County Health Department co.effingham.il.us/healthdepartment.html

Egyptian (IL) Health Department egyptian.org/

Evanston Health and Human Services cityofevanston.org/Departments/Health-HumanSvc

Fayette County (IL) Health Department fayettehealthdept.org/

Ford-Iroquois Public Health Department fiphd.org/

Franklin County - Williamson County Health Department bicountyhealth.org/

Fulton County (IL) Health Department fultoncountyhealth.com/

Hancock County (IL) Health Department hancockhealth.com/

Henderson County Health Department hendcohealth.com/

Henry & Stark County Health Departments henrystarkhealth.com/

Jackson County (IL) Health Department jchdonline.org/

Jasper County (IL) Health Department jasperhealth.org/

Jo Daviess County Health Department jodaviess.org/

Kane County (IL) Health Department kanehealth.com/

Kankakee County Health Department kankakeehealth.org/

Kendall County (IL) co.kendall.il.us/health.htm

Knox County Health Department knoxcountyhealth.org/

Lake County Health Department tinyurl.com/3fkgrqs

Lee County (IL) Health Department lchd.com/

Logan County Health Department logancountyhealth.org/

Macon County (IL) Health Department maconcountyhealth.org/

Madison County madisoncountyhealthdepartment.org/

Mason County (IL) Health Department masoncohealth.com/

McDonough County Health Department macomb.com/mchd/

McHenry County (IL) Health Department tinyurl.com/lnsryd

McLean County (IL) Health Department mclean.gov/Health/

Montgomery County Health Department montgomeryco.com/health/

Oak Park (IL) Public Health Department oak-park.us/Public_Health/Public_Health.html

Ogle County (IL) Health Department oglecountyhealthdepartment.org/

Peoria City County Health Department tinyurl.com/3ds45lt

Rock Island County Health Department co.rock-island.il.us/Health.aspx?id=156

Sangamon County Public Health Department scdph.org/

Southern Seven (IL) Health Department southern7.org/index.html

Springfield (IL) Public Health Department springfield.il.us/

Stephenson County Health Department co.stephenson.il.us/health/

Tazewell County (IL) Health Department tazewellhealth.org/

Vermilion County Public Health Department vchd.org/

Will County (IL) Health Department willcountyhealth.org/

Winnebago County (IL) Health Department wchd.org/

Whiteside County (IL) Health Department whitesidehealth.org/

Business license is handled at the county level.

Business Structure Filing: business.illinois.gov/registration.cfm

Business Name Registration: cyberdriveillinois.com/

Business Tax Registration: business.illinois.gov/registration.cfm

Small Business Administration Office: sba.gov/localresources/district/il/index.html

Indiana in.gov

Contact the Department of Health and your city or county in.gov/isdh/

Plan review form in.gov/isdh/files/SF50004_R3-6-05.pdf

Application for food service in.gov/isdh/files/SF49677_R5-05.pdf

Business Structure Filing: in.gov/sos/business/2381.htm

No state filing required for sole proprietorships

Business Name Registration:File with County Recorder in.gov/sos/business/2436.htm

Business Tax Registration: in.gov/dor/3963.htm

Information on Starting a Business: in.gov/ai/business

Small Business Administration Office: sba.gov/localresources/district/in/index.html

Indiana has a cottage foods law that enables you to sell baked goods at the Farmers Market and 'roadside stands.' Contact your health department for details. or:

Indiana State Department of Health

Phone: 317-233-7360

Email: food@isdh.in.gov

Iowa iowa.gov

Iowa Department of Inspections and Appeals, Food & Consumer Safety Bureau, 515/281-8587. Rules regulations and application are bundled together in download.

dia.iowa.gov/food/

No other license required

Business Structure Filing: sos.state.ia.us/business/

Business Name Registration: sos.state.ia.us/business/index.html

Business Tax Registration: idr.iowa.gov/CBA/start.asp

Information on Starting a Business: iowa.gov/Business_and_Economic_Development

Small Business Administration Office: sba.gov/localresources/district/ia

Iowa has a Cottage Law which allows home-based bakeries and food processing businesses. For details contact your local health department or the state Department of Agriculture.

tinyurl.com/3vkb9mb

Kansas kansas.gov

Kansas Department of Agriculture issues State Food Service License only. Health License, municipal occupancy permit, and building occupancy permits are issued at the city or county level. ksda.gov/records_center/content/286

Dept. of Agriculture: 785-296-7430

Food Code: kdheks.gov/pdf/regs/28-36.pdf

Business Name Registration: kssos.org/

Business Tax Registration: ksrevenue.org/busregistration.htm

Information on Starting a Business: in Kansas kssos.org/ fhsu.edu/ksbdc/

Small Business Administration Office: sba.gov/localresources/district/ks

Kentucky kentucky.gov

Cabinet for Health and Family Services, (502) 564-7181 chfs.ky.gov/

Contact local health department for licensing and inspection.

Business license:

You must register with the Department of Revenue revenue.ky.gov/business/register.htm

as well as obtain a local business license from your city or county department of revenue.

Business Structure Filing: sos.ky.gov/business/filings/

Business Name Registration: sos.ky.gov/business/filings/

Business Tax Registration: revenue.ky.gov/business/register.htm

Contact your city or county revenue department

Information on Starting a Business: kentucky.gov/business

Kentucky has a very restricted Cottage Food Law which allows its citizens to operate a home-based bakery. For details contact your local health department or the state Department of Agriculture. kyagr.com/

Louisiana louisiana.gov

Louisiana Dept. of Health, Food and Drug Division.

Requirements for food producers tinyurl.com/6xg97ar

Bakery specific regulations: tinyurl.com/3rj7lzc

Must have plans reviewed: tinyurl.com/3rgff2p

Step by step instructions: tinyurl.com/3qr6zxr

Business Structure Filing: sos.louisiana.gov

Business Name Registration: sos.louisiana.gov

Business Tax Registration: rev.louisiana.gov/sections/business/intro.aspx

Also contact your city or county revenue department

Information on Starting a Business: louisiana.gov/Business/Grow_a_Business/

Small Business Administration Office: sba.gov/localresources/district/la/index.html

Maine maine.gov

Dept of Agriculture , 207-287-3841

Application: maine.gov/agriculture/qar/qarforms/FoodandFuel-licenseapplication-2008.pdf

Business license issued through city/town

Business Structure Filing: maine.gov/sos/cec/corp/

Many municipalities require business registration. Check with your town/city clerk to find out about local regulations.

Business Name Registration: Not required

Business Tax Registration: maine.gov/cgi-bin/online/suwtaxreg/index

Also contact your city or county revenue department

Information on Starting a Business: in Maine maine.gov/portal/business/starting.html

Small Business Administration Office: sba.gov/localresources/district/me

Maine has a Cottage Law which allows its citizens to operate a home-based bakery. For more information about this law:

Quality Assurance and Regulation
28 State House Station Deering Bldg. – AMHI Complex
Augusta, ME 04333-0028
Hal Prince, Director
(207) 287-2161

extension.umaine.edu/onlinepubs/htmpubs/3101.htm

Maryland **maryland.gov**

Maryland Department of Health, Food Division 410-767-8400

Bakery and Kitchens regulated at the county level. State only regulates food processing plants.

Business license at county level. Must register trade name with state:

dat.state.md.us/sdatweb/nameappl.pdf

Business Structure Filing: dat.state.md.us/sdatweb/sdatforms.html#entity

Maryland Business Checklist dat.state.md.us/sdatweb/checklist.html#stru

Business Name Registration: dat.state.md.us/sdatweb/nameappl.pdf

Business Tax Registration: tinyurl.com/3fssbuo

Also contact your city or county revenue department

Information on Starting a Business: in Maryland tinyurl.com/8avbbp

Small Business Administration Office: sba.gov/about-offices-content/2/3120

Massachusetts **mass.gov**

Bakeries are regulated at the community level. You must contact your local health department for licensing and inspection. Business license and registration are also handled locally.

tinyurl.com/2jbjgl

Massachusetts Food Business Start Up Guide tinyurl.com/62mztxu

License application: mass.gov/Eeohhs2/docs/dph/environmental/foodsafety/food_app.pdf

Food Safety tinyurl.com/3rgxhrh

Information on Starting a Business: in MA tinyurl.com/2rar46

Small Business Administration Office: sba.gov/about-offices-content/2/3162

The state of Massachusetts has a Cottage law allowing its citizens to operate a home-based bakery. For details, contact your local health department or Massachusetts Department of Agriculture. mass.gov/agr/

MA Residential Kitchens: Questions and Answers:

http://www.mass.gov/eohhs/docs/dph/environmental/foodsafety/residential-kitchens-faq-brochure.pdf

"Starting a Wholesale Food Business in Massachusetts (PDF)

http://www.mass.gov/eohhs/docs/dph/environmental/foodsafety/start-wholesale-food-biz-tty.pdf

Michigan michigan.gov

Dept. of Agriculture. Food and Dairy Administration.

616-356-0609, mda-info@michigan.gov License and inspection handled at the regional level. The following link shows regions and links to get to their offices:

tinyurl.com/3bs3eoo

tinyurl.com/444v3o5

License application: tinyurl.com/3zrebu4

Business Structure Filing: tinyurl.com/63r6f8a

Business Name Registration: michigan.gov/sos

Business Tax Registration: tinyurl.com/3zpnrbx

Request a 518 Sales Tax Form. Also contact your city or county revenue department.

Information on Starting a Business: tinyurl.com/63r6f8a

Small Business Administration Office: sba.gov/about-offices-content/2/3121

Minnesota state.mn.us

All permitting and inspections handled through county. Must obtain sales tax license from the state.

Starting a Food Business in Minnesota tinyurl.com/3s7n5ds

Department of Agriculture, Food Division, 651-201-6027.

Facility requirements: tinyurl.com/3n436t3

Plan review application: tinyurl.com/6co4q6p

Wholesale business license: state.mn.us/license/content.do?mode=license&LicenseID=3930

Retail business license: state.mn.us/license/content.do?mode=license&LicenseID=4488

Business Structure Filing: sos.state.mn.us/index.aspx?page=92

Business Name Registration: sos.state.mn.us/index.aspx?page=92

Business Tax Registration: mndor.state.mn.us/tp/webreg.html

Also contact your city or county revenue department.

Information on Starting a Business: tinyurl.com/jjrob

Small Business Administration Office: sba.gov/about-offices-content/2/3121

Mississippi mississippi.gov/

All permitting and inspections handled through county.

State Dept. of Health msdh.state.ms.us/msdhsite/_static/30,3432,77,311.html

Regulations: msdh.state.ms.us/msdhsite/_static/30,0,77,60.html

Procedure flowchart: msdh.state.ms.us/msdhsite/_static/30,4098,77,311.html

Permit application: msdh.state.ms.us/msdhsite/_static/resources/432.pdf

No separate state business license required.

Business Structure Filing: tinyurl.com/MSBusiness

Business Name Registration: sos.ms.gov/business_services.aspx

Business Tax Registration: tax.ms.gov/regist.html

Information on Starting a Business: tinyurl.com/3asme4q

Small Business Administration Office: sba.gov/about-offices-content/2/3125

Mississippi bakers can sell their goods at Mississippi Farmers Markets. Certification is required. Participants may obtain certification by visiting the office of Richard C. Butler.

Contact: Richard C. Butler

Mississippi Farmers' Market

929 High Street

Jackson, MS 39202

Office: 601-354-6573

Fax: 601-354-7330

Email: RichardBu@mdac.state.ms.us

Missouri mo.gov

Department of Health. health.mo.gov/safety/foodsafety/faq.php

Inspections and licensing handled at county/local level.

Missouri food code: health.mo.gov/safety/foodsafety/foodcode.php

Must register fictitious business names with the state.

FAQ about registering: sos.mo.gov/business/corporations/fictitious_faq.asp

Contact information to request forms: (573) 751-4153, 1-866-223-6535

Business Structure Filing: sos.mo.gov/business/corporations/startBusiness.asp

Business Name Registration: sos.mo.gov/

Business Tax Registration: dor.mo.gov/business/register/

Information on Starting a Business: ms.gov/ms_sub_template.jsp?Category_ID=3

Small Business Administration Office: sba.gov/about-offices-content/2/3125

Missouri has a Cottage Law which allows home-based bakeries. For more information about this law, check with the county health department where you wish to sell your cakes. Also ask about specific requirements such as labeling

Find your county listing here: dese.mo.gov/moheritage/Counties.htm

Montana mt.gov

Dept. of Public Health, Food and Consumer Safety

dphhs.mt.gov/PHSD/Food-consumer/food-safe-index.shtml (406) 444-4735

Requirements of facility: tinyurl.com/3n25tyc

Montana rules: dphhs.mt.gov/index.shtml

Site plan approval requirements tinyurl.com/5v4vgxg

DPH issues license after inspection.

Business Structure Filing: sos.mt.gov/Business/index.asp

Business Name Registration: sos.mt.gov/Business/index.asp

Business Tax Registration: app.mt.gov/bustax/

Information on Starting a Business: mt.gov/business.asp

Small Business Administration Office: sba.gov/about-offices-content/2/3126

Nebraska nebraska.gov

Department of Agriculture, Bureau of Dairies and Foods, (402) 471-2536

Licensing handled by regional inspectors and regulations differ.

If outside Douglas and/or Lancaster County, 402-471-2536

If inside Douglas, 402-444-7480

If Inside Lancaster County, 402-441-6280

Business Structure Filing: sos.ne.gov/business/corp_serv/index.html

Business Name Registration: nebraska.gov/osbr/index.cgi

Business Tax Registration: revenue.state.ne.us/business/bus_regist.html

Information on Starting a Business: nebraska.gov/dynamicindex.html#

Small Business Administration Office: sba.gov/about-offices-content/2/3129

Nevada nv.gov

Department of Health, 775-684-4200

Bureau of Health Protections, Environmental Health

Food establishment rules: leg.state.nv.us/NAC/NAC-446.html

Plan review instructions: health.nv.gov/PDFs/feprapp.pdf

Business Structure Filing: nvsos.gov/index.aspx?page=415

Local Business license if sole proprietorship

Business Name Registration: nvsos.gov/

Business Tax Registration: nevadatax.nv.gov/web/

Information on Starting a Business: diversifynevada.com/

Small Business Administration Office: sba.gov/about-offices-content/2/3133

New Hampshire nh.gov

Rules: dhhs.nh.gov/dphs/fp/sanitation/

License application: dhhs.nh.gov/dphs/fp/sanitation/documents/fsapplication.pdf

Business Structure Filing: sos.nh.gov/corporate/

Business Name Registration: sos.nh.gov/corporate/tradenameforms.html

Business Tax Registration: nh.gov/revenue/faq/gti-rev.htm

Starting a Business in NH nheconomy.com/business-services/start-a-business-in-nh/

Small Business Administration Office: sba.gov/about-offices-content/2/3130

Home kitchen rules dhhs.nh.gov/dphs/fp/sanitation/documents/hkbrochure.pdf

New Jersey nj.gov

Dept of Health, 609-588-3123.

Regulations: state.nj.us/health/eoh/documents/chapter24_effective_1207.pdf

Wholesale license application: state.nj.us/health/forms/f-29.pdf

Business license: No state license for retail.

Business Structure Filing: state.nj.us/treasury/revenue/dcr/filing/leadpg.htm

Business Name Registration: state.nj.us/njbgs/njbgsnar.htm

Business Tax Registration: state.nj.us/treasury/revenue/dcr/filing/leadpg.htm

Also contact your city or county revenue department.

Information on Starting a Business: nj.gov/njbusiness/

Small Business Administration Office: sba.gov/about-offices-content/2/3131

New Mexico newmexico.gov/

Must submit plans for approval: nmenv.state.nm.us/fod/food_program/applications.html

Application for food permit: tinyurl.com/3h3tvtn

Business Taxes: tax.newmexico.gov/Businesses/Register-your-Business/Pages/Home.aspx

Also contact your city or county revenue department.

Information on Starting a Business: newmexico.gov/business.php

rld.state.nm.us/OS/PDF's/startingannmbusiness.pdf

Small Business Administration Office: sba.gov/about-offices-content/2/3132

New Mexico has a Cottage Food Law which allows home-based bakeries or food processing. For details contact your local health department or the state Department of Agriculture.

nmdaweb.nmsu.edu/

New York state.ny.us

Dept of Agriculture. Must be licensed. agmkt.state.ny.us/fs/general/license.html

License application: agmkt.state.ny.us/FS/license/pdfs/FSI-303.PDF

Business license issued at county level

Permits tinyurl.com/63453vn

Business Structure Filing: nysegov.com/citGuide.cfm?superCat=28

Business Name Registration: dos.state.ny.us/corps/bus_entity_search.html

Business Tax Registration: tax.ny.gov/

Information on Starting a Business: nysegov.com/citGuide.cfm?superCat=28

Small Business Administration Office: sba.gov/about-offices-content/2/3135

Some home processing is permitted: agmkt.state.ny.us/FS/consumer/processor.html

North Carolina ncgov.com

Commercial bakeries, cake shops, including catering operations, are regulated by county health departments (ncalhd.org/county.htm) and must meet the requirements of the North Carolina Rules Governing the Sanitation of Food Service Establishments (15A NCAC 18A .2600) deh.enr.state.nc.us/images/rules/t15a-18a.26.pdf

Permitting Information envhelp.org/pages/permit_coordination.html/

Plan review Unit deh.enr.state.nc.us/Food/plan2.htm

Business Structure Filing: secretary.state.nc.us/corporations/

Business Name Registration: thrivenc.com/smallbusiness/start-a-new-business

Business Tax Registration: dornc.com/forms/index.html

Also contact your city or county revenue department.

Information on Starting a Business: thrivenc.com/smallbusiness/start-a-new-business

Small Business Administration Office: sba.gov/about-offices-content/2/3127

North Carolina allows for a home-based bakery business.

Home-Based Guidelines: agr.state.nc.us/fooddrug/food/homebiz.htm

You must register with Dept of Revenue: tinyurl.com/3jxg7o2

Application for Home Processing Inspection: tinyurl.com/3fjhnrv

NC Department of Agriculture and Consumer Services

Food and Drug Protection Division

Food Regulatory Specialist

4000 Reedy Creek Road

Raleigh, NC 27607

919-733-7366

ncagr.com

North Dakota nd.gov

Dept of Health, Division of Food and Lodging. ndhealth.gov/foodlodging/

Regulations: tinyurl.com/6x9kmmo

Contact Food Division, 701-328-1291 for Plan Review Checklist. If your plan is approved, they will do an inspection followed by a license application.

Business Structure Filing: nd.gov/sos/businessserv/

Business Name Registration: nd.gov/sos/businessserv/registrations/tradename.html

Business Tax Registration: nd.gov/businessreg/

Information on Starting a Business: nd.gov/category.htm?id=160

Small Business Administration Office: sba.gov/about-offices-content/2/3128

Ohio ohio.gov

Licensing and inspections at county level. You must submit plans for approval prior to inspection.

Food Safety Certification tinyurl.com/3jpaqqu

Ohio Uniform Food Safety Code tinyurl.com/43ed9bl

Ohio Dept. of Agriculture
Division of Food Safety
8995 East Main Street
Reynoldsburg, OH
43068.

Phone: 614-728-6250, foodsafety@agri.ohio.gov.

Business Structure Filing: sos.state.oh.us/businessServices.aspx

Business Name Registration: business.ohio.gov/starting/

Business Tax Registration: business.ohio.gov/efiling/

Also contact your city or county revenue department.

Information on Starting a Business: business.ohio.gov/

Small Business Administration Office: sba.gov/about-offices-content/2/3138

Ohio has a Cottage Law which allows for a variety of foods to be home-produced, without the need for an inspected commercial kitchen. The new rules are available in a pdf document at the ODA web site: New Cottage Food Rules. tinyurl.com/3rfsus8

Licenses, Permits and Zoning ohioline.osu.edu/cd-fact/1201.html

Ohio Department of Agriculture Licensing tinyurl.com/3hvymgh

Oklahoma ok.gov

Licensing and inspections are handled at the county level.

Dept of Health. ok.gov/health/ or call 405-271-5243

Rules:

ok.gov/health/documents/Retail%20Foods257-2006.pdf

ok.gov/health/Protective_Health/Consumer_Protection_Division/

Business Structure Filing: okcommerce.gov/sbrs/

Business Name Registration: sos.ok.gov/corp/filing.aspx

Business Tax Registration: tax.ok.gov/bustax.html

Also contact your city or county revenue department.

Information on Starting a Business: ok.gov/section.php?sec_id=4

Small Business Administration Office: sba.gov/about-offices-content/2/3139

Oregon oregon.gov/

A plan review is required: oregon.gov/ODA/FSD/

egov.oregon.gov/ODA/FSD/docs/pdf/pub_pr.pdf.

They will then conduct an inspection. If the plan and inspection are approved, then an application will be completed at time of license issuance. Business license at county level.

Business Structure Filing: filinginoregon.com/

Business Name Registration: secure.sos.state.or.us/ABNWeb/

Business Tax Registration: oregon.gov/DOR/BUS/index.shtml

Also contact your city or county revenue department.

Information on Starting a Business: oregon.gov/menu_files/business_kut.shtml

Small Business Administration Office: sba.gov/about-offices-content/2/3140

Oregon has a Cottage Food Law which allows home-based bakeries or food processing. For details, contact your local health department or the state Department of Agriculture.

Domestic Kitchen website oregon.gov/ODA/FSD/program_food.shtml

Food Safety Division oregon.gov/ODA/FSD/faq_index.shtml

Phone: 503-986-4720

Email: fsd-expert@oda.state.or.us

Domestic Kitchens: oregon.gov/ODA/FSD/docs/pdf/pub_domkit.pdf

Labeling Requirements: oregon.gov/ODA/FSD/docs/pdf/pub_label_general.pdf

Pennsylvania pa.gov

The Pennsylvania Department of Agriculture (PDA) Bureau of Food Safety and Laboratory Services is responsible for enforcing food regulations and inspecting food establishments.

Contact the Pennsylvania Department of Agriculture or your local health department.

tinyurl.com/449c563

Business Structure Filing: tinyurl.com/3ppru5k

Business Name Registration:tinyurl.com/3ppru5k

Business Tax Registration: doreservices.state.pa.us/BusinessTax/PA100/FormatSelection.htm

Also contact your city or county revenue department.

Information on Starting a Business: pa.gov/portal/server.pt/community/work/3015

Small Business Administration Office: sba.gov/about-offices-content/2/3141

Pennsylvania has a Cottage Law which allows for home-based bakeries. For details contact your local health department or the state Department of Agriculture.

extension.psu.edu/food-safety/entrepreneurs/starting-a-business

Training and Resources extension.psu.edu/food-safety/events/topics/food-for-profit

Rhode Island ri.gov

Dept. of Health, Office of Food Protection. 401-222-2749

health.state.ri.us/licenses/food/

Business Structure Filing: sos.ri.gov/business/filings/

Business Name Registration: Businesses operating under an assumed name may be required to file an assumed name certificate with the city or town clerk .

health.ri.gov/records/about/clerkoffices/index.php

Business Tax Registration: ri.gov/taxation/BAR/

Also contact your city or county revenue department.

Information on Starting a Business: ri.gov/business/

Small Business Administration Office: sba.gov/about-offices-content/2/3144

South Carolina sc.gov/

Regulations are available from the Consumer Services Division of the South Carolina (S.C.) Department of Agriculture, which is responsible for enforcing safe food manufacture and sale at the state level: agriculture.sc.gov/foodsafetyandcompliance

Dept of Health and Environmental Control, Food Protection 803-896-0640.

Contact local Environmental Health office for permit application.

Business Structure Filing:: tinyurl.com/67ckdpk

Business Name Registration: scsos.com/Business_Filings_FAQs

Business Tax Registration: scbos.sc.gov/

Also contact your city or county revenue department.

Information on Starting a Business: sc.gov/business/Pages/default.aspx

Small Business Administration Office: sba.gov/about-offices-content/2/3145

South Dakota sd.gov

Dept of Health, 605-773-3361

Food service code: legis.state.sd.us/rules/DisplayRule.aspx?Rule=44%3A02%3A07

Application: doh.sd.gov/PDF/HPLICENS.pdf

Plan review questionnaire: doh.sd.gov/PDF/FOODSRV.PDF

Guidelines: doh.sd.gov/HealthProtection/guide.aspx

Step by step instructions: doh.sd.gov/HealthProtection/Food.aspx

Business license: contact Department of Revenue and Regulations, 605-773-3311

Business Structure Filing: tinyurl.com/3zneqxj

Business Name Registration: tinyurl.com/3gwdq94

Business Tax Registration: apps.sd.gov/applications/rv23cedar/main/main.aspx

Also contact your city or county revenue department.

Information on Starting a Business: sd.gov/servicedirect/

Small Business Administration Office: sba.gov/about-offices-content/2/3146

Tennessee tennessee.gov

Dept of Agriculture, Regulatory Services, Food and Dairy.

tennessee.gov/sos/rules/0080/0080-04/0080-04-11.pdf

Tennessee has a Cottage Food Law which allows home-based bakeries or food processing. For details, contact your local health department or TDA's Regulatory Services Division, Food and Dairy Section 615 837-5193.

Business Structure Filing: tn.gov/sos/bus_svc/corpFAQs.htm

Business Name Registration: tnbear.tn.gov/Ecommerce/NameAvailability.aspx

Business Tax Registration: tn.gov/revenue/tntaxes/business.htm

Also contact your city or county revenue department.

Information on Starting a Business: tn.gov/topics/Business

Small Business Administration Office: sba.gov/about-offices-content/2/3147

Texas texas.gov

Dept of State Health Services, Food and Drug Licensing.

Many cities and counties have local regulations; If no local regulations exist, then the state licensing is followed. Contact Food and Drug Licensing Department, 512-834-6626 for correct and up-to-date information. Due to the number of localities and the frequency of rule changes it will be the only place to get accurate updated information.

Business Structure Filing: sos.state.tx.us/corp/index.shtml

Business Name Registration: sos.state.tx.us/

Business Tax Registration: window.state.tx.us/taxinfo/sales/new_business.html

Also contact your city or county revenue department.

Information on Starting a Business: tinyurl.com/3mohenx

Small Business Administration Office: sba.gov/about-offices-content/2/3148

Texas has a Cottage Food Law which allows home-based bakeries or food processing. For details, contact your local health department or the state Department of Agriculture.

texascottagefoodlaw.com/

Utah utah.gov

Dept of Agriculture and Foods. 801-860-7075.

rules.utah.gov/publicat/code/r070/r070-560.htm

Food processing authorities: ag.utah.gov/divisions/regulatory/foodcompliance.html

Labeling guidelines: tinyurl.com/6dkfqg7

One-stop licensing and registration for business license:

secure.utah.gov/osbr-user/user/welcome.html

Business Structure Filing: utah.gov/business/starting/structure_starting.html

Business Name Registration: utah.gov/business/starting/structure_starting.html

Business Tax Registration: tax.utah.gov/business/information

Also contact your city or county revenue department.

Information on Starting a Business: business.utah.gov/

Small Business Administration Office: sba.gov/about-offices-content/2/3154

Utah has a Cottage Food Law which allows home-based bakeries or food processing. For details contact your local health department or the state Department of Agriculture.

le.utah.gov/~code/TITLE04/htm/04_05_000905.htm

Food Compliance: ag.utah.gov/divisions/regulatory/foodcompliance.html

Vermont vermont.gov

Bakery rules: healthvermont.gov/enviro/food_lodge/Bakeries.aspx

License application:

healthvermont.gov/enviro/food_lodge/documents/food_lodge_application.pdf

Business license may also be required from county.

Business Structure Filing: sec.state.vt.us/corps/corpindex.htm

Business Name Registration: sec.state.vt.us/corps/forms/tradeapp.htm

Business Tax Registration: vermont.gov/portal/business/index.php?id=91

Also contact your city or county revenue department.

Information on Starting a Business: vermont.gov/portal/business/

Small Business Administration Office: sba.gov/about-offices-content/2/3156

Vermont has a Cottage Food Law which allows home-based bakeries or food processing. For details contact your local health department or the state Department of Agriculture.

Apply for a License: healthvermont.gov/forms/documents/JULY_2008_APP.pdf

vermontagriculture.com/

vermontagriculture.com/agdev/documents/farmersMarketRegulations.pdf

Virginia virginia.gov

Contact the Department of Agriculture and Consumer Services. 804.786.3520

Business Structure Filing: scc.virginia.gov/clk/begin.aspx

Business Name Registration: scc.virginia.gov/clk/index.aspx

Business Tax Registration: tax.virginia.gov/site.cfm?alias=BusinessHome

Also contact your city or county revenue department.

Information on Starting a Business: portal.virginia.gov/business/

Small Business Administration Office: sba.gov/about-offices-content/2/3155

Washington wa.gov

Dept. of Agriculture 360-902-1876, *Lucy* 360-273-6777

Information regarding facility requirements: agr.wa.gov/foodanimal/foodprocessors/

Agriculture 'green book,' contains some information that may be useful:

agr.wa.gov/Marketing/SmallFarm/directmarketinghandbook.aspx

Hardcopies of all handbooks and forms available by calling 360-902-1876 and requesting "food processors packet."

Business licensing guide: call 360-664-1400 or bls.dor.wa.gov/

Business Structure Filing: sos.wa.gov/corps/Default.aspx

Business Name Registration: bls.dor.wa.gov/

Business Tax Registration: dor.wa.gov/content/doingbusiness/registermybusiness/

Also contact your city or county revenue department.

Information on Starting a Business: access.wa.gov/business/start.aspx

Small Business Administration Office: sba.gov/about-offices-content/2/3157

Washington has a Cottage Food Law which allows home-based bakeries or food processing. For details, contact your local health department or the state Department of Agriculture.

Annual inspections of cottage food operations to be conducted by the Washington State Department of Agriculture, (WSDA), or by a local health jurisdiction under contract with the WSDA.

The maximum annual income of a cottage food operation is $12,000.

The fees associated with a cottage food permit are $125 for inspection, $30 for processing, and $75 for public health review.

West Virginia wv.gov

Inspection and permitting of food establishments are the responsibility of the local health department. wvdhhr.org/phs/food/index.asp

Business Structure Filing: sos.wv.gov/Pages/default.aspx

Business Name Registration: sos.wv.gov/Pages/default.aspx

Business Tax Registration: wva.state.wv.us/wvtax/default.aspx

Also contact your city or county revenue department.

Information on Starting a Business: business4wv.com/b4wvpublic/default.aspx

Small Business Administration Office: sba.gov/about-offices-content/2/3159

West Virginia has a Cottage Food Law which allows home-based bakeries or food processing. but you are limited to selling your products at state approved Farmers Markets. For details contact your local health department or the state Department of Agriculture.

smallfarmcenter.ext.wvu.edu/farmers_markets/vendor_resources

ehs.wvu.edu/r/download/48045

Wisconsin wisconsin.gov

All license information found here including where to request application packet:

foodsafety.wisc.edu/food_business_licensing.html

Food Business Innovation in Wisconsin: fyi.uwex.edu/foodbin/the-food-bin-network/

Business Structure Filing: wdfi.org/corporations/forms/

Business Name Registration: wisconsin.gov/state/byb/name.html

Business Tax Registration: revenue.wi.gov/faqs/pcs/btr-on.html

Also contact your city or county revenue department.

Information on Starting a Business: wisconsin.gov/state/core/business.html

Small Business Administration Office: sba.gov/about-offices-content/2/3158

Wisconsin has a Cottage Food Law which allows home-based bakeries or food processing. For details contact your local health department or the state Department of Agriculture.

Starting a small food business in Wisconsin

fyi.uwex.edu/farmersmarkets/files/2009/05/small_business_FactSheet0812.pdf

Food Safety Regulations:

foodsafety.wisc.edu/assets/pdf_Files/Brouchure_on_Starting_a_Small_Business-DATCPNov09.pdf

Wyoming wyoming.gov

Dept of Agriculture, Consumer Protection. Facility requirements:

wyagric.state.wy.us/divisions/chs/food-safety

Business Structure Filing: soswy.state.wy.us/Forms/FormsFiling.aspx?startwith=Business

Business Name Registration: soswy.state.wy.us/Forms/FormsFiling.aspx?startwith=Business

Business Tax Registration: tinyurl.com/6bk6bju

Also contact your city or county revenue department.

Information on Starting a Business wyomingbusiness.org/program/starting-a-business/3413

Small Business Administration Office: sba.gov/about-offices-content/2/3160

Wyoming has a Cottage Food Law which allows home-based bakeries or food processing. For details contact your local health department or the state Department of Agriculture.

wyagric.state.wy.us/

legisweb.state.wy.us/2009/Introduced/HB0016.pdf

Credits

"House" symbol by Adam Iscrupe, from The Noun Project collection.

"Pencil" symbol by Gina R. Furnari, from The Noun Project

"Cake" symbol by The Noun Project collection

"Whisk" symbol by Richard Clarke, from The Noun Project

"Graphic Design" symbol by Anna Weiss, from The Noun Project

"Radio Tower" symbol by John Caserta, from The Noun Project

"Coffee" symbol by Maximilian Becker, from The Noun Project

"Cupcake" by Julia Soderberg, from The Noun Project

"Community" symbol by Rémy Médard, from The Noun Project collection

"Food Mixer" by Simon Child, from The Noun Project

Checklist symbol by Michael Young, from The Noun Project

Security (badge)Thibault Geffroy, from The Noun Project

For more information and downloads visit us online:

http://cake-business.com/resources/

Made in the USA
Lexington, KY
20 September 2014